CAMPAIGN • 228

TEUTOBURG FOREST AD 9

The destruction of Varus and his legions

MICHAEL McNALLY

ILLUSTRATED BY PETER DENNIS

Series editor Marcus Cowper

First published in Great Britain in 2011 by Osprey Publishing,
Midland House, West Way, Botley, Oxford OX2 0PH, UK
44-02 23rd St, Suite 219, Long Island City, NY 11101, USA
Email: info@ospreypublishing.com

Osprey Publishing is part of the Osprey Group.

© 2011 Osprey Publishing Ltd

A CIP catalogue record for this book is available from the British Library.

ISBN: 978 1 84603 581 4

Ebook ISBN: 978 1 84908 308 9

Editorial by Ilios Publishing Ltd, Oxford, UK (www.iliospublishing.com)
Page layout by: The Black Spot
Index by Sandra Shotter
Typeset in Sabon and Myriad Pro
Maps by Bounford.com
Battlescene illustrations by Peter Dennis
Originated by PDQ Media
Printed in China through Worldprint Ltd.

11 12 13 14 15   12 11 10 9 8 7 6 5 4 3

AUTHOR'S NOTE

Firstly, and as always, I'd like to thank my wife, Petra, and children – Stephen, Elena and Liam – for their help, patience and understanding whilst I was working on the manuscript. Again, thanks to Andy Copestake, Martin Francis, Seán Ó Brogaín, Lee Offen and Ian Spence for their proofreading of the text in its various incarnations as well as to Marcus Cowper, my editor, for his continued support and to Peter Dennis who has once again produced superlative artwork to illustrate specific incidents during the battle. I would also like to take this opportunity to thank Dr Joseph Rottmann and the staff of the Varusschlacht Museum and Park at Kalkriese both for their kind hospitality during my visit to the battlefield and also for their kind assistance in answering a number of my subsequent queries, Angelika Pirkl of AKG images for helping to source a number of images reproduced within the book and finally Tony Clunn who was kind enough to take the time to discuss his initial discoveries at Kalkriese.

This book is therefore respectfully dedicated to Major (Retd.) Tony Clunn OBE without whom the story of the battle of the Teutoburg Forest – the *Varusschlacht* – would most likely have remained shrouded in the mists of historical legend.

Please note that unless otherwise accredited, all images are from the author's personal collection.

ARTIST'S NOTE

THE WOODLAND TRUST

Osprey Publishing are supporting the Woodland Trust, the UK's leading woodland conservation charity, by funding the dedication of trees.

www.ospreypublishing.com

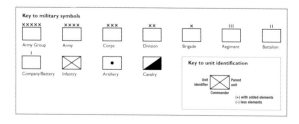

CONTENTS

The Roman Empire under Augustus, *c.* AD 9

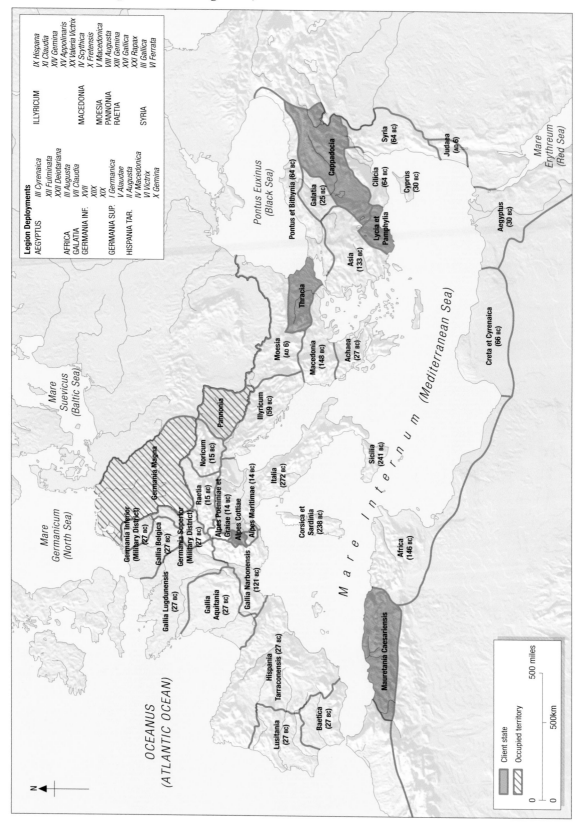

Legion Deployments

AEGYPTUS	III Cyrenaica
	XII Fulminata
	XXII Deiotariana
AFRICA	III Augusta
GALATIA	VII Claudia
GERMANIA INF.	XVII
	XIIX
	XIX
GERMANIA SUP.	I Germanica
	V Alaudae
HISPANIA TAR.	II Augusta
	IV Macedonica
	VI Victrix
	X Gemina
ILLYRICUM	IX Hispana
	XI Claudia
	XIV Gemina
	XX Valeria Victrix
MACEDONIA	IV Scythica
	X Fretensis
MOESIA	V Macedonica
PANNONIA	VIII Augusta
RAETIA	XIII Gemina
	XVI Gallica
SYRIA	XXI Rapax
	III Gallica
	VI Ferrata

Pontus Euxinus (Black Sea)

Mare Suevicus (Baltic Sea)

Mare Germanicum (North Sea)

Mare Internum (Mediterranean Sea)

Mare Erythreum (Red Sea)

OCEANUS (ATLANTIC OCEAN)

Syria (64 BC)
Judaea (AD 6)
Cappadocia
Cilicia (64 BC)
Cyprus (30 BC)
Aegyptus (30 BC)
Pontus et Bithynia (64 BC)
Galatia (25 BC)
Lycia et Pamphylia
Asia (133 BC)
Creta et Cyrenaica (66 BC)
Thracia
Moesia (AD 6)
Macedonia (148 BC)
Achaea (27 BC)
Illyricum (59 BC)
Pannonia
Sicilia (241 BC)
Italia (272 BC)
Noricum (15 BC)
Raetia (15 BC)
Germania Magna
Germania Inferior (Military District) (27 BC)
Gallia Belgica (27 BC)
Germania Superior (Military District) (27 BC)
Alpes Poeniniae et Graiae (14 BC)
Alpes Cottiae
Alpes Maritimae (14 BC)
Corsica et Sardinia (238 BC)
Africa (146 BC)
Gallia Lugdunensis (27 BC)
Gallia Aquitania (27 BC)
Gallia Narbonensis (121 BC)
Mauretania Caesariensis
Hispania Tarraconensis (27 BC)
Lusitania (27 BC)
Baetica (27 BC)

N

Client state
Occupied territory

0   500 miles
0   500km

INTRODUCTION

During the political upheavals of the mid-19th century it was inevitable that countries would begin to look back into their history in order to seek a figure to define their modern national identity. For France this role was filled by Vercingetorix, the Gallic war-leader defeated by Caesar at the siege of Alesia in 52 BC. The German States, however, took for their inspiration Arminius, a chieftain who had not merely resisted Rome but had also annihilated a force of three Roman legions at the battle of the Teutoburg Forest in AD 9, or as it became more readily known *die Varusschlacht* – the Varus battle – so named after the Roman commander who perished alongside his men.

Because of Caesar's detailed commentaries the site of Alesia was well known, and in 1865 a statue of Vercingetorix was erected on the heights overlooking the town of Alise-Sainte-Renne, and it was intended that the place become a focal point for the study of France's Gallic past. For the Germans, however, although the fact of their battle was uncontested, its actual location remained shrouded in mystery and, until it was identified, no similar memorial could be considered. Subsequently much time and ink were spent debating the location of their ancestors' triumph and, eventually, the search narrowed down to an area around the town of Detmold in the southern portion of the Teutoburg Forest.

In 1841 work began on a 52m-tall (170ft) monument above the town, on the summit of the Teutberg, the 385m-high (1,263m) eminence which gives the forest its name. As a sign of German unity, funds were contributed by all of the German States, but eventually monies ran out and the project was completed only in 1875 when Prussia settled all outstanding costs. Tellingly enough, the statue was not built facing south, as a gesture of defiance against Arminius' historical enemies, the Romans, but rather westwards, towards Prussia's main Continental rival – France.

This, the accepted orthography of the *Varusschlacht* was not to remain unchallenged, and over the years a number of prominent scholars advanced their own ideas about the location of the battle. One such was Theodor Mommsen (1817–1903) who placed the battle much further west, near the hamlet of Kalkriese. Mommsen based his theory partially on a significant number of Roman coins – none of which antedated the Emperor Augustus – which had been found, over the course of several generations, on land belonging to the Bar family. But more tellingly Mommsen believed that the Latin term used by Tacitus *Saltus Teutoburgensis*, commonly translated as 'Teutoburg Forest' could also be read as 'Teutoburg Gap'. Mommsen argued that this could mean that the climactic engagement took place within the

LEFT
Some 27m (90ft) tall, and resting on a cupola of a similar height, the Hermann Denkmal, towers above the valley below. The sheer scale of the edifice can be seen by comparing it with the people on the viewing platform that runs below the dome of the cupola. (AKG Images)

RIGHT
Theodor Mommsen (1817–1903). One of the foremost German scholars to consider alternative locations to Detmold as being the site of the *Varusschlacht*, Mommsen's theory gained much ground during the 20th century and formed the basis for later excavation of the Kalkriese site.

confines of a narrow pass such as that at Kalkriese rather than in the wooded area propounded by his contemporaries. Despite his pre-eminence as a scholar, Mommsen's theory remained just one of a number of alternative locations for the battle, the case against which was eloquently put forward by the historian Hans Delbrück in the second volume of his study of politico-military history *Geschichte der Kriegskunst im Rahmen der politischen Geschichte – Teil II: Die Germanen* (Berlin, 1921), which deals with the conflict between Rome and the Germanic peoples.

It is more than probable that Mommsen's theory might have remained exactly that but for Lieutenant Tony Clunn who, in 1987, was a British officer stationed with the Royal Army Medical Corps in Osnabrück. Hoping to pursue his twin hobbies of metal detecting and Roman History, Clunn contacted the regional chief archaeologist, Dr Wolfgang Schlüter, hoping to receive permission to conduct a search of the area for Roman artefacts. Schlüter agreed to his request, and pointed him to the area of Kalkriese near the Bar estate.

Slowly, Clunn's methodical approach began to bear fruit, resulting in his crucial first find – a silver denarius dating from the reign of the Emperor Augustus – the same period as the Varus disaster. Other, more numerous, coin deposits were subsequently found, but, although encouraging, they were inconclusive as definite evidence of a Roman presence in Kalkriese. The breakthrough itself, however, came in the summer of 1988 when Clunn found a number of lead slingshot. As a weapon, the sling was not used by the Germanic tribes, but was however commonly used by Roman auxiliary forces. The discovery of such missiles in the area was therefore concrete proof that, at some stage, Roman troops had fought an engagement in or around Kalkriese, possibly vindicating Mommsen's theory about the location of the *Varusschlacht*.

Major (Retd) Tony Clunn OBE.
(Tony Clunn)

ROME AND THE GERMANS

Perhaps the first real encounter between Rome and the Germanic peoples came towards the end of the 2nd century BC, when two tribes, the Cimbri and the Teutones migrated southwards from the Jutland Peninsula. By 113 BC they had crossed the river Danube and entered the lands of a Celtic tribe, the Taurisci. Unable to repel the invaders, the Taurisci appealed to Rome for assistance and the Senate duly dispatched an army to induce the tribesmen to return whence they came. But when the Roman commander, having achieved his objectives, exceeded his orders and attacked the retreating columns as they passed the town of Noreia, his army was cut to pieces.

Eight years later, the tribesmen marched into Gallia Narbonensis where two Roman armies – over 80,000 men – were mobilized to defend the province. The opposing forces met near the town of Arausio, but disunity within the Roman high command precluded any chance of joint action and they were defeated in detail. With catastrophe looming, Gaius Marius – a veteran soldier – was elected senior consul and legislation enacted that would allow him to extend his term of office in order to prosecute the war. In short, the Senate was prepared to give Marius as much time as was needed to place the army in a state of readiness to defeat the enemy.

Approaching Italy, and with the countryside unable to support their vast numbers, the tribes split into two columns with the Teutones marching along the coast whilst the Cimbri crossed the Alps. Although based upon logistical necessity, it was nonetheless a flawed decision and diluted effectively the numerical advantage that had seen the Germans victorious so far. Given that theirs was the easiest route, Marius moved first against the Teutones and defeated them comprehensively at Aquae Sextiae, having previously ordered his consular colleague Quintus Lutatius Catulus to mount a forward defence and occupy the alpine passes in order to block the Cimbrian passage into northern Italy. Inexplicably, however, Catulus declined to follow orders and instead fell back across the river Po.

Taken from a late 19th-century German atlas, this map shows a slightly politicized view of the northern frontier of the Roman Empire as it appeared in the century following the Varus disaster. Here Germania Magna extends as far east as the Vistula and the Polish border, encompassing all of 'Greater Germany' – the Wilhelmine Second Reich – and not just those territories known to have been occupied by Rome.

Marching west, Marius assumed overall command of both Roman armies and took up position near the town of Vercellae, where he planned to fight a decisive engagement. Although the terrain suited both armies, it was in fact the Roman heavy cavalry which decided the battle before it began by launching a devastating attack as the tribesmen were still forming up for battle. In the ensuing fighting, an estimated 400,000 Cimbrians were either captured or killed before the remnants of the tribe were able to escape the carnage.

The German threat averted, a grateful Republic quietly forgot about these tribesmen from the north until some decades later, when a Gallic tribe – the Sequani – invited a Suebian chieftain, Ariovistus, to fight for them against the Aedui, a rival tribe allied to Rome. Rewarded with a grant of land, from his victorious allies, Ariovistus repopulated his new lands with increasing numbers of his countrymen and was soon strong enough to turn upon the Sequani, forcing them to cede him almost two-thirds of their territory. Alarmed by this ever-growing Germanic presence so close to its borders, the Senate in Rome attempted to mollify the Suebian leader by conferring on him the title *socius et amicus populi Romani* 'ally and friend of the Roman people' whilst simultaneously instructing the governor of Gallia Narbonensis – Gaius Julius Caesar – to protect Aeduan interests at all costs.

Ambitious in the extreme, Caesar's plans to attack Ariovistus were stalled by the advent of the Helvetii, a Celtic tribe living in the Alps who, under pressure from their neighbours to the east, had marched into Aedui territory in the hope of establishing a new homeland there. In this instance Caesar was not only obliged to act in support of his allies' interests, but also, perhaps more importantly, to fill the dangerous vacuum which the Helvetii had left behind them, an area into which the very neighbours from whom they had fled could march unchallenged and from there threaten Roman territory.

Caesar crushed the migrants in a short and decisive campaign and, in accordance with his remit from Senate, his peace terms were simple and reflected a desire to return to the *status quo ante bellum*. He required merely that the Helvetii return to their original homeland and rebuild their settlements, effectively closing the border to any further incursions. He was now free to deal with the Suebii, whom he attacked and defeated heavily near Vesontio, before forcing them back across the Rhine.

By now many tribes, discerning their fate if Rome were able to engage them piecemeal, banded together for mutual support but Caesar moved quickly, aiming to pick off the members of the Confederation one at a time, thereby keeping them off balance and retaining the initiative. As his campaign progressed, the threat posed by the Germans across the Rhine became an increasing problem and when, in 56 BC, the resurgent Suebii drove two other tribes – the Tencteri and the Usipati – into Gaul, Caesar was forced to act.

As subsequent negotiations with the tribes stalled, and deciding that the time for diplomacy was at an end, Caesar arrested their leaders and then launched a surprise attack on their camp, after which, according to his own narrative, 'Our men returned to camp without a single fatal casualty and with only a very few injured, after fearing that they would be involved in a very difficult campaign since the enemy had numbered 430,000'. Many of the Germans drowned, attempting to flee across the Rhine, and those who survived sought the protection of another tribe, the Sugambri, who, when ordered to hand over the fugitives to Roman justice, ominously replied that the Rhine was the limit of Roman power, and that She had no right to dictate how affairs were conducted east of the great waterway. Stung by this impertinence, Caesar led a punitive expedition across the river, but the enemy simply melted into the forests and remained there until he was forced to return to Gaul, thus foregoing any possible victory, east of the Rhine.

Unrest continued during Caesar's absences in Britain during 55/54 BC, and upon his return he cut a bloody swathe through the north of the country, restoring Roman rule. The political climate was changing, however, and these reprisals became a pretext for the Gauls – including Rome's erstwhile allies, the Aedui – to rise up in revolt. The fate of the province hung in the balance until 52 BC, when Caesar captured the Gallic leader Vercingetorix after the successful siege of Alesia. Conscious of the fact that his term of office was soon to expire, and determined to leave a pacified Gaul behind him, Caesar embarked upon a final destructive campaign against the Eburones, killing many of the tribe and consigning even more to slavery, before returning to Italy in 50 BC to deal with his enemies in the Senate.

It is perhaps a corollary of the personal nature of Caesar's detailed commentaries that, in his absence, we know very little about the military situation in Gaul during the Civil War. What is certain, however, is that the garrison units were heavily drawn upon to provide manpower for the main theatre of operations, leaving only a skeleton force *in situ* manning a series of encampments along the Loire and Sâone valleys. However, with the advent of the Second Triumvirate (43–33 BC), and the establishment of a more stable government in the Roman world, attention was once again focused on the Republic's northernmost territories.

With the final showdown between Octavian and Mark Antony coming at Actium in 31 BC, troops were again withdrawn from the province, and once again the tribes rose up in a revolt which raged unchecked until 28 BC. The following year Octavian, now known as *Princeps Augustus*, visited Gaul and divided the country into three smaller provinces: Gallia Aquitania, Gallia Lugdunensis, and Gallia Belgica, roughly equating to the south, the centre and the north respectively of the original province. In addition to this division, Augustus also created two military districts to cover the Rhine (Rhenus) frontier: Germania Superior and Germania Inferior. It should be stressed that these administrative divisions were not provinces in their own right, being created from the easternmost portion of Gallia Belgica, but were in fact intended as a buffer zone to protect the newly reorganized Gallic provinces from the Germans across the Rhine.

This reorganization in the north firmly underlines the strategic importance of the Rhine Valley, and as such the need for swift communications between Rome and the frontier became an increasingly important factor in the development of imperial strategy. Accordingly, the next stage in Augustus' plan was to be the formal annexation of the Alpine regions that commanded the direct land route between Gaul and the Italian Peninsula. In 15 BC, in a classic pincer movement, Roman armies led by Augustus' stepsons Drusus and Tiberius mounted a swift campaign that added two new provinces to the Empire.

Despite the increased governmental involvement, military deficiencies within the Gallic provinces became starkly apparent in 16 BC when Marcus Lollius, governor of Gallia Belgica, was heavily defeated by the Sugambri, and the *aquila* (eagle) of *legio V Alaudae* captured. In itself, this was not an insurmountable disaster, as the standard was soon retaken, but as the century drew to a close, it served as an uncomfortable reminder of the relative impunity with which the Germanic tribes could attack Rome's northernmost province. It also brings into question the exact nature of Augustus' policy with regard to Germania. One school of thought believes that he intended to pin Rome's northern borders upon a recognizable terrain feature, in this case the

These two iron 'dolphin'-shaped hooks were to fix the doubling of the legionary's *lorica hamata* in place, thus providing him with added shoulder protection in combat. The inscriptions indicate that they were the property of a soldier named Marcus Aius who was a member of his cohort's first century, and that his commanding officer was called Fabricius – 'M.Aii I (centuria) *Fab*(ricii) / M.Aius I (centuria) *Fabrici*(i)'. (AKG Images/Varusschlacht Museum, Kalkriese)

river Rhine, whilst a second theory is that the situation was much more fluid, as the army units in the area were ultimately used not only to defend against external aggression, but also to maintain the rule of law within the existing provincial structure. Accordingly, by 12 BC the Gallic legions were now redeployed in a series of newer, forward bases such as Moguntiacum (Mainz), Fectio (Vechten), Novaesium (Neuss) and Vetera (Xanten) which were themselves supported by a chain of smaller forts garrisoned by auxiliary units.

Planning for a campaign in Germany across the Rhine now began in earnest, with Augustus appointing his younger stepson Drusus as effective governor of all three Gallic provinces as well as the German military districts and giving him a force of six legions supported by a considerable number of auxiliary troops. Early in the year, Drusus launched a pre-emptive strike against the Sugambri, advancing deep into their territory before conducting an orderly withdrawal to the Rhine. His next action was to compel the Frisii, a tribe whose territory encompassed the mouth of the Rhine, to submit to Rome, and, using the camp at Fectio as his headquarters, his then troops cut a waterway from the Rhine to the Ijsselmeer enabling warships to transit from the Rhine to the North Sea with ease, thus giving him a considerable strategic edge over his opponents. Whilst a number of demonstrations were made from the Rhine bases, the bulk of Drusus' forces now embarked on the fleet and sailed for the mouth of the river Ems (Amisia), presumably to land a considerable force in the enemy's rear.

Despite the audacity of the plan, it ground to an ignominious halt when the fleet ran aground leaving it at the mercy of both tide and tribesmen. Indeed it was only the arrival of a force of newly allied Frisian warriors that saved both Drusus' pride and his army. With the campaigning season drawing to a close, the Roman commander withdrew into winter quarters to begin planning operations for the following year. Faced with what was obviously a determined Roman effort to establish a presence on the right bank of the Rhine, three of the larger German tribes – the Cherusci, the Suebii and the Sugambri – formed an anti-Roman alliance, which, even if it had originated as a defensive measure, could also be seen as an offensive or even provocative undertaking, as it soon became known that the three tribes had between them agreed a tentative division of any spoils before a sword had been drawn.

The fractured political situation in Germania Magna was soon illustrated when the Sugambri invited a neighbouring tribe – the Chatti – to join the alliance; the Chatti demurred, preferring an alliance with Rome. In the spring of 11 BC, the two tribes found themselves at war and, with the Sugambri thus occupied, Drusus crossed the Rhine and, having scattered the Usipati, drove east towards the river Weser and Cheruscan territory, where he spent several months attempting to bring the enemy to bay before a lack of supplies compelled him to withdraw towards the Rhine. On the return journey, the army came under continual attack from the Cheruscans, and indeed at one stage the column ominously had to fight its way out of a narrow defile whilst engaged from all sides. In this instance, superior discipline, and above all, an exceptionally gifted commander allowed the Romans to break out of the trap and reach safety. In order to maintain a presence in hostile territory that could be used as a springboard for offensive future operations, Drusus established a number of small garrisons and then withdrew back across the Rhine.

The following year, it suddenly appeared that the previous campaigns had all been for naught, as the Chatti repudiated their alliance with Rome and joined the hostile coalition. Deciding to make an example of these 'oath breakers', Drusus based his army at Moguntiacum and ravaged their lands, but, despite the massive destruction, he was unable to crown his campaign with a decisive engagement. In 9 BC, however, he was able to secure a hitherto elusive victory over the Chatti and then moved against the Marcomanni, driving them eastwards into Bohemia. The Hermandurii were the next of the tribes to feel the weight of his sword and, seemingly unstoppable, he continued this chain of successive victories by turning on the Cherusci, leading one of his contemporaries to comment wittily that the whole campaign was not in fact conducted in pursuit of imperial policy but rather in order to gratify Drusus' desire to kill a German chieftain in single combat and dedicate the captured arms and armour at the temple of Jupiter First and Greatest in Rome.

Having settled matters with the Cherusci and taken a number of hostages, Drusus then pushed on towards the Elbe (Albis), turning south along the valley of the river Saale (Salla) and fighting a number of small actions along the way, before eventually beginning the final phase of the expedition that would bring his army back to its winter quarters on the Rhine. Somewhere along the march however, he broke his leg in a riding accident and gangrenous complications set in which were to prove fatal. Rome's most successful campaign in Germany to date had led ultimately to the death of her most able commander.

In 8 BC, Drusus' elder brother Tiberius, a capable general in his own right, was appointed to the command in Germany and launched his own attack against the Sugambri and their allies. This was, perhaps, the high water mark of the Roman occupation of Germany as, although no territorial annexation had been announced, it was plain to see that the imperial writ, in the words of Colin Wells, 'extended as far as her arm could reach'. In other words, with superior mobility aided by semi-permanent forward camps and the advantages conferred by her complete naval superiority, Rome's control now stretched further into Germania Magna than ever before. Tiberius' command in Germany was fated not to last long and in 6 BC he fell into imperial disfavour, going into voluntary exile on the island of Rhodes. It would seem that the period immediately following Tiberius' exile was merely one of consolidation, but one of his successors, the former consul Lucius Domitius Ahenobarbus, having suppressed a number of local uprisings, notably marched his army from Moguntiacum to the Elbe, traversing the river and erecting a trophy on the eastern bank as a tribute to Roman arms, the first and perhaps the last of her generals to cross this major waterway.

As the 1st century BC drew to a close, the new-found prosperity of the region seemed to engender a dangerous complacency in Rome. Not only was there now a thriving cross-border economy, but the fact that a number of the tribes had elected to become allies gave an impression of pacification bolstered by the large numbers of Germanic warriors willing to enlist as auxiliary troops in the Roman Army. As the events of AD 9 gradually unfolded, this complacency would have fatal consequences for the Empire.

CHRONOLOGY

113 BC   Cimbri and Teutones cross the Danube, defeating a Roman army at Noreia.

105 BC   The tribes enter Gallia Narbonensis, defeating the Romans at Arausio.

104 BC   Gaius Marius elected senior consul.

103 BC   Marius' consulship extended.

102 BC   Marius defeats the Teutones at the battle of Aquae Sextiae.

101 BC   Marius defeats the Cimbri at the battle of Vercellae.

62 BC   The Sequani engage the Suebii under Ariovistus to attack the Aedui.

60 BC   Aedui defeated by the Sequani. The Suebii settle in Gaul.

59 BC   Ariovistus recognized as 'ally and friend of the Roman people'.

58 BC   Helvetii cross into Gaul seeking a new homeland but, defeated by Caesar, are forced to return to their former homes.

57 BC   Northern Gallo-German tribes unite against Caesar but are defeated at the battle of the river Sabia.

56 BC   Caesar crosses the Rhine and conducts inconclusive campaign in Germany.

53 BC   Gallic tribes rise in revolt under the Avernian chieftain Vercingetorix.

52 BC   Caesar besieges Alesia and captures Vercingetorix.

46 BC   Assumed date for birth of Varus.

44 BC   Assassination of Caesar.

43 BC   Formation of Second Triumvirate.

31 BC	Octavian defeats Antony at Actium, effectively becoming ruler of Rome.
27 BC	Division of Gallia Comata (Long-haired Gaul) into three provinces. Creation of the German military districts.
18 BC	Assumed date for birth of Arminius.
16 BC	Lollius defeated by the Sugambri.
15 BC	Alpine tribes conquered by Drusus and Tiberius.
13 BC	Varus elected consul.
12 BC	Drusus begins the first of three years of successive campaigns in Germania Magna.
9 BC	Death of Drusus.
8 BC	Tiberius assumes command in Germany, defeats the Sugambri. Varus appointed governor of Africa.
7 BC	Varus appointed governor of Syria.
3 BC	L. Domitius Ahenobarbus crosses the Elbe.
AD **7**	Varus appointed commander of the German military districts.
AD **9**	Destruction of the Army of Germania Inferior by German tribes under Arminius.
AD **11**	Tiberius appointed commander of the German military districts.
AD **13**	Germanicus appointed commander of the German military districts.
AD **14/16**	Germanicus campaigns in Germania Magna.
AD **14**	Legionary *aquila* recaptured from the Marsii.
AD **15**	*Aquila* of *legio XIX* recaptured from the Bructeri.
AD **16**	Germanicus defeats Arminius at the battle of Idistaviso.
AD **41**	Remaining legionary *aquila* recaptured from the Chaucii.

OPPOSING COMMANDERS

This marble copy of a statue of Augustus, taken from the Villa Livia, shows a youthful and virile emperor, confident in his martial glory. At the time of the battle, he would have been in his early 70s, having ruled supreme for over four decades. The breastplate worn here by the emperor shows the return – in 20 BC – of the legionary standards captured by the Parthians from Crassus (53 BC) and Mark Antony (40–38 BC). (AKG Images/Nimatallah)

PUBLIUS QUINCTILIUS VARUS (*c.*46 BC–AD 9)

Although the exact date is unknown, Varus was born sometime during the 40s BC, the only son of Sextus Quinctilius Varus a prominent member of the Pompeian faction during the Civil War who committed suicide after the battle of Philippi in 42 BC rather than be attainted for treason.

Despite spending his childhood in the care of various relatives, it would appear that the young Publius successfully embarked on the *cursus honorum*, the path of public service as, in 22 BC, he was appointed as *quaestor Augusti* to the Emperor Augustus during the latter's three-year tour of the eastern provinces. Ordinarily, Varus would have been eligible for this office only at the age of 30, but as this appointment was in the purview of the Imperial Crown, the age requirement would seem to have been waived. In any event it would seem to indicate that the Civil War loyalties of his family were not held against him.

Returning to Rome, Varus continued his upward rise, combining a political career with military service, and in 15 BC he commanded *legio XIX* in Noricum and Raetia, his tenure of command possibly extending through to the conquest of the alpine provinces the following year. With the campaign brought to a successful conclusion, a strategic marriage strengthened his social position and the following year he was elected junior consul, colleague of his former commanding officer Tiberius Claudius Nero, the emperor's stepson.

In 8 BC Varus was appointed governor of the senatorial province of Africa, where he was widely acknowledged as having discharged his duties creditably, and the following year was appointed governor of Syria. Arguably the most important posting in the Eastern Empire, the incumbent had to walk a political tightrope, having not only to maintain the political status quo with Parthia to the east, but also having to keep a number of client rulers in line. It was a task for neither the inexperienced nor the fainthearted and Varus proved his mettle when he decisively intervened to resolve the succession crisis following the death of Herod the Great of Judaea in 4 BC.

Varus' tenure of office in Syria gives us two contradictory images of the man. For the Jewish historian, Flavius Josephus, writing several decades later, and possibly in an attempt to smooth over political tension in the Judaea of his own day, Varus is a capable soldier and able diplomat, whilst to Velleius Paterculus, a contemporary, 'He came to a rich province a poor man, but left a poor province a rich man', clearly an inference of corruption and malfeasance. His gubernatorial duties resolved, Varus then married for the third and final time, to Claudia Pulchra – Augustus' great-niece – thus firmly cementing his position within the Imperial inner circle, presumably remaining in Rome until his appointment to the German command in AD 7.

ARMINIUS (*c.*18 BC–*c.* AD 21)

Much like his adversary little is known of Arminius' early life. He was born possibly around 18 BC, eldest son of Segimer, an influential nobleman of the Cherusci, a Germanic tribe whose homeland was in the valley of the river Weser (Visurgis), near the modern city of Minden. Following Drusus' crushing victory over the tribe in 8 BC it was inevitable that Segimer's heir would be amongst those children taken hostage to assure the tribe's future good behaviour, and during his time in Rome Arminius would undoubtedly therefore have undergone the same education as would any aristocratic Roman of the same age.

This marble bust from the Capitoline Museum in Rome is a stylized, heroic representation of the Cheruscan leader. With a leonine mane of wavy hair it is similar in pose to known likenesses of both Alexander the Great and Pyrrhus of Epirus, indirectly comparing Arminius to both of these great generals in an effort to mitigate the shock of defeat. (AKG Images)

As a member of the military caste, and despite his youth, Arminius would no doubt have taken two memories with him as he prepared to enter the enemy's lair. Firstly, the ambush in 11 BC in which the Cheruscans – possibly led by his father – had trapped Drusus' army in a defile and inflicted heavy casualties before the Romans could extricate themselves, and secondly Drusus' successful campaign of 8 BC which after shattering Cheruscan resistance had in fact led to his being taken to Rome. The moral derived from both incidents is that the Romans could be defeated, but only in a situation where their tactical flexibility and discipline could not be brought to bear. He resolved therefore, to learn everything that he could about his mortal enemy, searching for a weakness that could one day be turned to his advantage.

Coming of age, Arminius was admitted into the *ordo equester* – the equestrian order – which facilitated his commission as an officer of auxiliary troops. In AD 4 he is known to have served in Pannonia and here may have met Valleius Paterculus, the future historian, who at this time was serving with the army as a prefect of auxiliary cavalry.

Now in his early 20s, and perhaps outwardly seeming more Roman than the Romans themselves, Arminius returned to his people, ready to assume his position as his father's heir – the perfect ambassador to convey the benefits of friendly relations with Rome to the Cherusci. It is unknown whether he remained in military service at this time or later simply re-enlisted, but his place as a hostage was assumed by his younger brother Flavius who would have presumably been too young to suffer from the anti-German backlash that was to pervade Rome in the aftermath of the Varian disaster.

Having destroyed the Army of Germania Inferior in AD 9, Arminius was initially forced onto the defensive by Germanicus' ultimately unsuccessful campaigns of AD 14–16 and subsequently fought an inconclusive war against Maroboduus of the Marcomanni, but with neither able to secure a military advantage, a stalemate ensued. In AD 21 tribal rivals poisoned him, possibly members of his own immediate family who were reputedly becoming alarmed at his increasing autocracy.

OPPOSING ARMIES

THE ROMANS

At the time of his appointment as Imperial Legate in the military district of Germania, Varus had under his command a total of five legions supported by an unknown number of auxiliary units, perhaps equal to 20 per cent of Rome's front-line strength. Only Illyricum, again with five legions, contained a garrison of a similar size.

Germania itself was subdivided into two areas of operations. In the north, Germania Inferior was commanded by Gaius Numonius Vala with a principal garrison of three legions – *legio XVII* at Novaesium, *legio XIIX* at Vetera and *legio XIX* at Oppidum Ubiorum (Cologne) whilst in the south, Germania Superior under Lucius Nonius Asprenas – one of Varus' nephews – was garrisoned by the *legio I Germanica* and *legio V Alaudae* both based at Moguntiacum. Thus, linked by a chain of smaller outposts manned by auxiliary units, the main legionary concentrations covered the valleys of the Lippe (Luppia) in the north, and the Main (Moenus)/Wetter in the south, which by this time had developed into the traditional routes of attack into the interior of Germania Magna.

During the early Imperial period, each legion was composed of 10 sub-units or *cohortes*, each further divided into six centuries (*centuriae*) of 80 soldiers and 20 servants apiece, commanded by a centurion, and giving each legion a paper combat strength of 4,800 men supported by 120 'legionary' cavalry whose main tasks comprised scouting and escort duty. Throughout the early Principate, a cadre of veterans – effectively serving a second enlistment – was often added to the legion establishment and, although it is unclear if this practice still existed in the latter part of Augustus' reign, its presence may have been the stimulus for the expansion of the legion's first cohort during the reign of Vespasian (AD 69–79).

The legionary's primary offensive weapon was a heavy javelin (*pilum*) whose metal shank was specially designed to bend on impact and render enemy shields unwieldy and useless in combat. It could also not be re-used by the enemy and, after the fighting was over, the least damaged would be straightened out by legionary blacksmiths and reissued to the troops. The legionary's secondary weapons were a short stabbing sword (*gladius*) and a wide-bladed dagger (*pugio*).

Roman Coolus-type helmet, early 1st century AD. Perhaps the most common form of legionary headgear, the hemispherical copper-alloy bowl was surmounted by a knob to hold a horsehair crest and reinforced by a number of riveted sections for additional protection. In this example the neck and face guards can be plainly seen, as can the rivets and hinge that would have held the cheek-guards in place.

For defence, legionaries of this period relied on a large cropped rectangular shield held in the left hand, a bronze or iron helmet, predominantly of the Coolus type, and most importantly a mail shirt (*lorica hamata*) worn over a padded over-tunic and a woollen undergarment. Until recently it was generally believed that this was the only type of body armour used by soldiers of the Augustan period, but excavations at Kalkriese have since uncovered several partial examples of a form of articulated armour – *lorica segmentata* – more commonly associated with the army of the middle and late 1st century AD.

In combat, the technique used was that the *pilum* was discharged just as the opposing forces came into contact, disrupting the cohesion of the enemy line before the legionaries closed and engaged the enemy with their *gladii* in short economical thrusts intended to kill or incapacitate their opponents whilst they effectively cut their way into the opposing formation, more often than not using their shield bosses as an ancillary weapon with which they made a sweeping punch in order to knock their opponents off balance, thus rendering them a better target for a decisive sword thrust.

During the reign of Augustus, the legions were generally supported by locally raised troops known as *numeri*, often supplied by allies or client states in units of no fixed size or composition led by their own officers or nobles and best described as 'irregulars'. These troops were dressed and equipped exactly as the warriors of their own nation. With the subsequent reduction in the size of army from the 60 or so legions in existence at the time of Actium to the 26 of the early empire, the number of front-line troops had decreased to around 140,000 or so effectives and thus a new solution needed to be found that would allow Rome to meet her military commitments, but at a fraction of the cost of wholly employing citizen soldiers or the locally raised *numeri*.

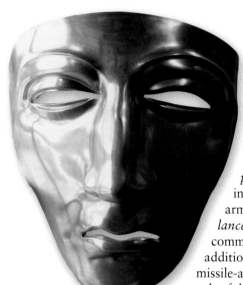

Augustus, therefore, introduced a relatively new type of soldier, the *auxiliarius* (lit. 'helper') who, drawn from the ranks of the disenfranchised subjects of the empire, would be rewarded with citizenship upon their honourable discharge at the end of their enlistment. The auxiliaries were equipped and organized along regular lines into *cohortes* (infantry) and *alae* (cavalry) both types of unit being suffixed by the terms *quingenaria* denoting the unit size i.e. 500 men (although in practice they would have contained 480 effectives) and either *pedita* or *equitata* which described the unit's role as either infantry or cavalry. In the main, these troops would have been armed and equipped similarly to the legionaries, but carrying the *lancea* a lighter spear or javelin instead of the *pilum* and more commonly a round or oval shield in place of the legionary *scutum*. In addition to the previously mentioned units, there were also specialist missile-armed units such as archers or *sagittarii* who, like the auxiliary cavalry fulfilled a role in which the citizen soldiers were deficient.

Modern research has shown that the numbers of auxiliaries in service during the early empire were roughly equal to those of the legionaries, and thus it has been accepted as a rule of thumb that the number of legionary cohorts and auxiliary units in existence were equal, although whether or not this was strictly adhered to on a regional basis remains theoretical. However, it does provide a plausible overview of the size of the German garrison. With a total of five legions deployed within the military district, this would equate to an additional 50 or so auxiliary units, which dwarfs the known number of such formations that accompanied Varus on his march into the interior of Germania Magna, a discrepancy that can readily be explained by the fact that a large proportion of these troops would not only have been employed in manning the existing series of camps, but also in garrisoning a number of

ABOVE
As visitors enter the main exhibition hall of the Varusschlacht Museum, they are greeted by a massive reconstruction of a Roman parade mask, which has become the museum's logo.

RIGHT
For added protection, legionaries carried a large semi-rectangular shield made of several layers of wood glued together and faced with a decorative covering of painted leather reinforced with iron fittings. Here we have the boss (*umbo*), which was often used offensively in combat, together with the grip (*ansa*) and the edging that protected the shield's rim from damage. (AKG Images/Varusschlacht Museum, Kalkriese)

locations at least within Gallia Belgica, but possibly within all three of the Gallic provinces. This would also explain why, in the wake of the disaster, Asprenas felt able to march north with a significant proportion of the Moguntiacum legions; something that he would not have been able to do had the local defences in Germania Superior been undermanned.

Varus' command

The size of the Roman column destroyed by Arminius has obviously been the subject of lengthy discussion, with the numbers of combatants and noncombatants generally ranging anywhere from 20,000 to 30,000 based not only on the known units that were involved but also a 'variable' added to represent wives and families as well as the inevitable civilians that would – in theory at least – have accompanied an army on the march.

In order to come to a realistic estimate of the size of Varus' command in the summer of AD 9 we need to make a number of important assumptions, the first being that the winter camp (*castrum hibernum*) of each of the three legions was garrisoned by a single cohort and secondly that the units themselves were not at full strength. For this exercise a nominal deduction of 10 per cent should be assumed for detachments, casualties, sick, etc., which would give each legion a campaign strength of approximately 4,360 men supported by perhaps 1,200 noncombatant servants, thus a combined total for the three legions of 16,680 of all types.

Despite the lack of a formal regimental structure, the auxiliary units would have mustered – at full strength – approximately 480 soldiers with 20 servants, and thus, under the criteria expressed above, the nine units attested to would have come to approximately 3,888 soldiers and 162 servants. When combined with the above estimate for the legions, this would yield an estimated combat strength at the beginning of the campaign of 17,000 effectives supported by 3,800 noncombatants, both totals being eroded by the need to make further detachments and establish additional garrisons in order to maintain communications with the Rhine bases as the column pushed ever further into Germania Magna.

According to Cassius Dio (Book 56, Ch. 20) Varus' column also included a large number of civilians: 'They had with them many wagons and pack animals, as they would for a journey in peace time; they were even accompanied by women and children and a large retinue of servants.' What must be borne in mind is that Dio was writing over two centuries after the battle (AD 211–33), and that in this single sentence he makes a number of important wrong assumptions that have coloured how Varus' column has been regarded over the last two millennia.

Firstly, and dealing with each of the comments in turn, the legion's transport echelon was effectively based upon the number of units present down to the last century, which – assuming that the whole legion was present – would be exactly the same irrespective of time of year or whether the legion was operating in friendly or hostile terrain.

Next, Augustus introduced a prohibition on marriage within the army, possibly enacted at the same time as he reduced the total number of legions. The reasoning behind this ban was that as the new legions were intended to be flexible in terms of strategic deployment – those on the Rhine, for example,

Roman auxiliary cavalryman's helmet, early 1st century AD. This trooper's helmet has been sculpted so as to resemble human hair surmounted with laurel leaves, and would have been overlaid with metal leaf to add to this impression. Unlike the legionary helmet, the face guard is largely ornamental, whilst both the neck and cheek guards are larger and more flared and pronounced, assisting in protecting the ears without inhibiting the wearer's ability to hear orders or trumpet calls.

More like open-toed marching boots than sandals, and designed for both comfort and durability, the remnants of these Roman *caligae* clearly show the number of hobnails or studs used to ensure the legionary a secure footing both on the march and in combat. (AKG Images/Varusschlacht Museum, Kalkriese)

were to be ready for deployment not only within Germany, but also within the Gallic provinces – they should not be burdened with the families and dependants of the rank and file whilst on active service. It should be noted, however, that the ban was not extended to senior officers as their appointments were often political in nature and in any event much shorter than the regular legionary enlistments, and as a quid pro quo they were given adequate enough leave for them to visit their families and not vice versa. Although later emperors introduced legislation to ameliorate the effects of the marriage ban, it should be noted that it remained in force until the reign of Septimius Severus (AD 193–211), who died, coincidentally, as Dio was commencing his work.

Finally, and as has been seen above, the provision of noncombatant servants was a standard feature of the legion's organizational structure and thus any 'excess' could have come only from the suite of Varus in his role as Augustus' legate in Germany, but, even allowing for the tastes of a member of the imperial inner circle, it is highly doubtful that he would have been attended by a significant enough number of servants to warrant Dio's comment.

Given that the troops were going to be on campaign for a number of months and would not be returning to their winter camps until the autumn, a number of the more ambitious or avaricious of the merchants who plied their trades from the small communities or *canabae* that grew up on the edges of the Rhine bases would have undoubtedly accompanied the column in the anticipation of a profitable summer but, in comparison with the number of troops under arms, their numbers would have been minimal – most likely only numbering in the hundreds – again being in no way sufficient to support Dio's observation.

THE GERMANS

Unlike their adversaries, and given the nature of their society, the Germans have regrettably left no written record which can be used to quantify the size of Arminius' forces in AD 9. Accordingly, historians have resorted to various demographic studies in order to gain a rough idea of the population of Germany at the time and then to use these results as a basis upon which to estimate the number of fighting men available. The problem is that – dependent upon the criteria used – the results vary greatly.

In one of the more recent narratives of the battle, Adrian Murdoch (*Rome's Greatest Defeat*) suggests that Arminius commanded a force of approximately 25,000 men, which would have comfortably outnumbered Varus' army. Murdoch also attempts to identify the tribes that took part in the battle, adding the Angrivarii and Bructeri to Arminius' own Cheruscans. Another modern author, Peter Wells (*The Battle that Stopped Rome*), paints a larger canvas and on the assumption that Arminius' forces came from all tribes within a radius of 80km (50 miles) of Kalkriese, suggests that he would possibly have had anywhere between 17,000 and 100,000 warriors under his command. Despite this broad range, Wells states that possibly 18,000 warriors would have taken part in the final stages of the battle around the Kalkrieser Berg.

At first glance, Wells' assumptions are reasonable enough – he is indeed following a similar methodology to that used by the late Dr John S. Gray in *Centennial Campaign: The Sioux War of 1876* (University of Oklahoma Press: Norman, OK, 1988) in which Gray calculated the number of Sioux and Cheyenne warriors at the Little Big Horn by multiplying the known number of Indian lodges with a demographic breakdown of the inhabitants of each lodge. Wells's approach is similar but there are two variables which he omits from his calculations; the first is quite simply the fact that, as per the example of the Cheruscan leaders Segestes and Segimer, many tribes were divided in their feelings towards Rome, and secondly the fact that for several years the Romans had waged a series of bloody campaigns across Germania Magna resulting in numerous casualties on both sides, and whilst the Romans had a significant manpower reserve on which they could draw in order to mitigate these losses, the Germanic tribes had no such facility and could only wait upon natural population growth in order to resolve any manpower shortage.

eroberung · machtübernahmen
conquest · assumption of power

Reconstruction of Germanic warrior, early 1st century AD. Typical of the bulk of Arminius' forces, this German warrior is relatively under-equipped when compared with his main adversary. Wearing a linen or woollen tunic with woollen trousers and a heavy, fringed cloak of the same material, his main armament is a long spear that would most likely have been reserved for hand-to-hand combat rather than for use as a missile weapon, whilst a dagger hangs from his belt, obscured here by the folds of his cloak. (Jona Lendering)

Roman Imperial-Gallic-type helmet, early to mid-1st century AD. An iron helmet more commonly associated with legionaries of the early empire, this model is beginning to show more pronounced neck and cheek protection than the earlier Coolus type, as well as decoration in the form of bronze plates on the cheek guards. (AKG Images/Erich Lessing)

Going even further back, Delbrück estimates that – on average – each German tribe would have had between 6,000 and 8,000 fighting men, adding understandably that the larger tribes would have had correspondingly more men under arms and the smaller ones correspondingly less. Given what we know of the three tribes through whose territory Varus marched, this would also give a possible German strength of between 20,000 and 30,000 warriors to which calculation, when discussing the personal retinues of the tribal chiefs, Delbrück adds the codicil that 'In designating these ruffians as professional warriors, however, we must be careful not to think of the other Germans as farmers; there is only a difference of degree. All are warriors.' The importance of this comment is that here we have a secondary source purposely differentiating between the minority of well armed and well equipped fighting men within each tribe, and the greater majority whose armament would have been either more simple or even improvised – perhaps a hunting spear or a woodsman's axe and whose protection would have been limited to a light wooden or wickerwork shield. Indeed the term *nudus* as employed by Tacitus on a number of occasions although often translated as 'naked' can also be taken as meaning 'unarmoured' which thus makes perfect sense in describing this general levy of the tribes.

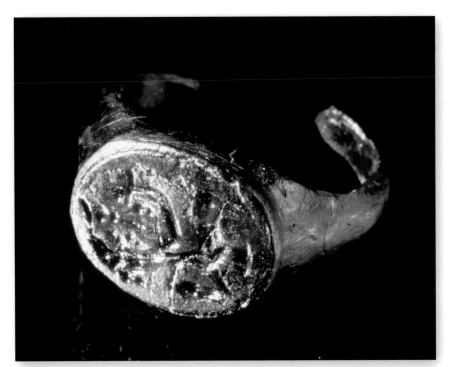

The hard core of Arminius' army would have been centred around the personal followers of the individual tribal chieftains, men whose sole business was warfare and who may have thus have been used as an assault force or to stiffen the less motivated levies. Their clothing and equipment would have been more extensive than that of the rank and file. As his primary weapon, each would most likely have carried a *framea*, a spear that could be used either as a missile weapon or in hand-to-hand combat, supplemented by a number of lighter javelins. In addition to this they may have carried swords or light axes as secondary weapons with a dagger or hunting knife as a weapon of last resort. Clothing would have consisted of woollen trousers tied at the ankle and belted at the waist, over which was worn a woollen or linen tunic, over which may have been worn a heavy woollen cloak that would double as a blanket. Hair would have been commonly worn either pulled back into a topknot or pinned at the side of the head in a 'Suebian' knot. Body armour, in the form of a mail shirt, was rare and when worn would have been undoubtedly either the spoils of war or the result of service as a Roman auxiliary. Finally, a round or hexagonal shield would have completed the warrior's equipment.

ORDERS OF BATTLE

Roman

Regretfully, contemporary sources are vague not only about the size of Varus' army but also about its composition, referring solely to the units that were destroyed during the running combat and not the actual number of troops that set out from Vetera in March AD 9.

It is as a result only of indirect references, such as the Caelius Tombstone or the fact that the numbers of three legions were removed from the army list towards the end of Augustus' reign that historians have been able to identify the major units involved.

> *legio XVII*
> *legio XIIX*
> *legio XIX*
> Six auxiliary *cohortes* 'quingenaria pedita'
> Three auxiliary *alae* 'quingenaria equitata'

Each of the legions would probably have fielded no more than 4,600 effectives, whilst the auxiliary units, more than likely composed of Gauls or 'West Bank' Germans would themselves have possibly had a field strength of 450 men each.

German

Using Delbrück as a guide, the initial number of troops available to Arminius would have been as follows:

> Angrivarii, *c.*5,000 men
> Bructeri, *c.*8,000 men
> Cherusci, *c.*8,000 men

To these should, theoretically, be added warriors from tribes such as the Marsii, Sugambri, and Usipati through whose lands the Romans had constructed their route into the interior of Germania Magna, who would have possibly doubled Arminius' force had they accepted his command rather than acting independently against Roman outposts within their tribal areas such as Aliso (Haltern).

OPPOSING PLANS

VARUS IN GERMANIA

BELOW LEFT
This wooden model of a *gladius* scabbard shows the relative position of various metal fittings discovered on the battlefield. (AKG Images/ Varusschlacht Museum, Kalkriese)

BELOW RIGHT
This interesting-looking key was for the lock of a Roman strongbox, possibly either that of one of the army's pay chests or perhaps part of Varus' personal baggage or that of one of his senior officers. (AKG Images/Varusschlacht Museum, Kalkriese)

Citing ancient sources such as Paterculus, Tacitus and Dio, many modern commentators tend to support the belief that Varus, whatever his political abilities was a military incompetent who had been charged with the creation of Trans-Rhenal Germany – Germania Magna – as a province of Rome and that his failure to succeed in this task not only contributed to his death and the destruction of the greater part of Rome's forces in the region, but also led to the establishment of the Rhine as Rome's north-eastern frontier.

The accuracy of this perspective, however, leaves several questions unanswered, all of which have a material bearing on any discussion of Varus' success or failure. The first is that his appointment is dated from approximately AD 6/7 which, unless personally extended by the emperor, would have expired three years later, at the latest in AD 10, i.e. one year after the disaster in which he lost his life. In these first years of his tenure it would therefore appear that Varus did nothing whatsoever to fulfil any brief to create a new province as none of the Roman sources available to us cites the implementation of any measures that would signify the creation of a central governmental authority.

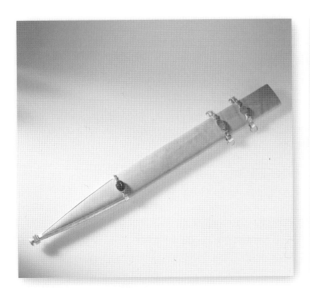

The pacification of Germania Magna

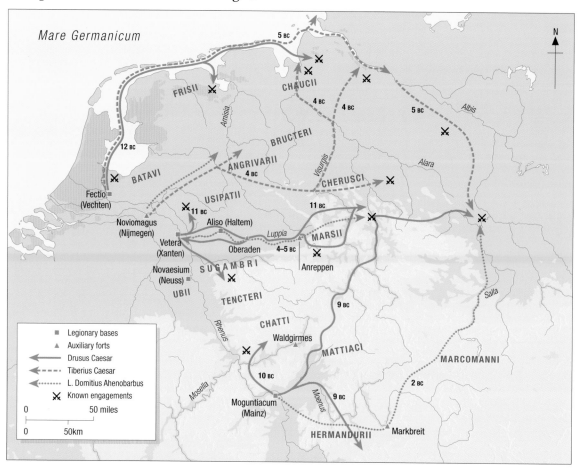

In Varus' Germany there were indeed a number of major roads and a few fledgling towns such as Oppidum Ubiorum (Cologne), but it must be remembered that these were all on the left bank of the Rhine and, politically speaking, part of Gallia Belgica. With the possible exception of the settlement at Waldgirmes near Wetzlar, which might in fact antedate the *Varusschlacht*, there are no traces of the establishment of the bureaucratic hub required for the day-to-day running of an imperial province. In addition, it has been stated that much of Varus' time during the summer of AD 9 was spent collecting taxes from the Germanic tribes, and yet, under Augustus, Rome had changed the manner in which taxes were collected. The *publicani*, the tax farmers and speculators of the late Republic, were now a thing of the past, having been replaced by more efficient methods underpinned by a census of a province's population. There is no record of such a survey having been taken in Trans-Rhenal Germany. Indeed with roughly half of the population under the yoke and temporarily acquiescent and the remainder allied to Rome but still independent, it is difficult to see how such an undertaking could have been carried out.

More likely is that, given what we know of Varus' time in Germany, he was sent there not as a soldier but as a result of his political ability. What Augustus needed was a man on the spot who could not only be trusted to act responsibly and decisively when required, but who had also had experience of dealing with the type of stubborn factionalism prevalent within the Germanic tribes. In short, his brief was not to conquer Germania Magna, but rather instead to reinforce the status quo – to reassure the allied tribes that their loyalty to Rome was in no way misplaced, thus preventing defections and ensuring that those tribes that had been beaten into submission during the campaigns of his predecessors remained subservient.

In order to achieve this he relied on similar tactics to those used by the British on the North-West Frontier of India almost two millennia later – regular processions through the disputed territory intended to display the might of Rome. In this he was aided by a number of pro-Roman nobles such as Segestes of the Cherusci whose cause was, ultimately, doomed to failure. For whilst it will remain uncertain how such loyalty to Rome came about, Varus had at this time a more reliable and trustworthy source of intelligence with regard to this, the most warlike of German tribes – a man who on one hand was the heir to one of the most important of the Cheruscan chieftains, but on the other had been educated and spent most of his life in Rome, a man who was not only a member of the equestrian order, but who had also recently served with distinction as an officer of auxiliaries. In short, he placed his confidence in a cavalry prefect named Arminius and as a result fatefully ignored a number of warnings, a failing that would lead him ultimately to disaster.

This small cache of 19 Roman coins (15 denarii, three quinarii and a gold aureus) all minted during the 1st century BC was uncovered from the battlefield. The quinarius also known as the 'half denarius' had been reintroduced as legal tender in 118 BC and was used almost exclusively within Gaul, illustrating that its owner would have been stationed or employed within the Gallic provinces. (AKG Images/ Varusschlacht Museum, Kalkriese)

ARMINIUS

As the son of a Cheruscan chieftain, Arminius would have heard and seen how the Romans were vulnerable to his tribe's methods of waging war when they could be lured into unfavourable terrain and denied the ability to manoeuvre. He would also be aware of the running engagements between the Romans and the Sugambri, where the latter employed 'hit-and-run' tactics to harass the enemy before melting into the protection of the forests.

It will never be known when Arminius decided to turn upon Rome. The catalyst may have been a decision made during his gilded incarceration or the result of something witnessed during his service in Pannonia. It could even have been due to an unrecorded incident that occurred after his return to Germania Magna. Having served alongside the legions for a number of years he would have had a perspective unique amongst his peers, for rather than merely being the target of Roman attacks, he would have been involved in their planning and implementation of such operations. In short he would have seen and understood the rationale behind how the Romans waged war against the barbarian tribes.

Given the paucity of contemporary sources available to us, we must assume that Varus' actions in the summer of AD 9 followed a more or less established pattern and thus Arminius could make his plans accordingly. The first thing that he needed to do would be to contact chieftains known to be hostile to Rome and establish his bona fides as, for want of a better phrase, a German patriot. This was the most crucial and the most dangerous aspect of the whole plan as, without the support of other tribes, even the united Cherusci could not hope to defeat Varus' forces alone, and the longer he took to marshal his allies the greater would be the chance of his plans being betrayed to the enemy.

Fully aware that he could not conduct a protracted campaign, Arminius decided that any combat would need to be resolved quickly and decisively before the qualitative superiority of the Roman forces could become a decisive factor as it had two decades earlier. His plan was therefore based upon three factors: firstly upon the Romans' belief that they were operating in either friendly or pacified territory; secondly in his ability to persuade Varus to make his summer camp, *castrum aestivum*, within Cheruscan territory where it could be closely observed; and finally to persuade the legate to remain longer in camp than was usual by pandering to his perceived mission of 'romanization'. The longer that Varus could be delayed from returning to the winter camps, *castra hiberna*, along the Rhine, the potential for unrest among the tribes would be greater.

Utilizing the fact that Varus' force would contain a large baggage train, what Arminius needed was to find an area where the proposed route westwards narrowed sufficiently so that small forces could block Roman forward and rearward movement trusting that – effectively tied to the baggage – the main body would remain relatively immobile, a suitable target for a series of localized harassing attacks. He found his potential ambush site near Kalkriese. There the pathway along the northern slopes of the Wiehengebirge meandered through a bottleneck created by a large area of marsh and bogland to the north – das Grosse Moor – and the high ground of the Kalkrieser Berg to the south. It is highly doubtful that, at this stage, Arminius believed that his plan would result in a comprehensive Roman defeat but a victory, any victory, would be the best way in which to consolidate his position, not only within the Cherusci but also with those tribes who, however quiescent they may have outwardly seemed, had always remained hostile to Rome.

THE CAMPAIGN

THE MARCH TO THE WESER

BELOW LEFT
Attached to the top of the shaft, these *pila* ferrules were used to affix the slender, flexible head to the main body of the weapon. Made of iron, these examples are approximately 5cm (2in.) in length. (AKG Images/Varusschlacht Museum, Kalkriese)

BELOW RIGHT
As the legionaries' primary offensive weapon, the *pilum* was designed to bend on impact and thus render the enemy's shields useless. The section behind the point is clearly bowed, showing how it would have been rendered useless after impact. (AKG Images/Varusschlacht Museum, Kalkriese)

Over the winter of AD 8/9, Publius Quinctilius Varus, *legatus Augusti pro praetore*, the Imperial representative in Germany sent a number of couriers with instructions for his senior subordinates. These orders were of two distinct types: firstly the instructions were for the commanders of *legiones XVII* and *XIX* to arrange for garrisons, possibly one cohort at each location, to be left to secure their winter camps and then for the remainder of each formation to march to Vetera in order to unite with the rest of the army. For the auxiliary troops, a number of units were ordered to march directly for Vetera, whilst the remainder were redeployed in order to use the reduced local strength best to meet the security requirements of both the military district and the Gallic provinces. Whilst these preparations were under way, a courier was also sent to Moguntiacum with orders for Lucius Nonius Asprenas instructing him firstly to continue his observation of the Chatti, once allied to and now opposed to Rome, as well as to maintain a watching brief on the activities of Maroboduus of the Marcomanni whose armed neutrality could easily escalate into open hostility should he ever scent a Roman weakness that could be converted to his own advantage.

Varus' plan, such as it was, was simple. From Vetera, the army would cross the Rhine and once on the eastern bank enter the valley of the river Lippe, traditionally the route used by Roman forces marching into the interior

of Trans-Rhenal Germany. Following the river, and supported by elements of the *Classis Germanica*, a small riverine fleet based at Vetera which would carry supplies and heavy equipment, the troops were to march eastwards along the line of outposts established by Varus' predecessors, a number of which were still in service and which would be resupplied and their garrisons rotated as the column passed. Once the upper reaches of the Lippe had been traversed, the troops would then strike north-east, further into the lands of the Cherusci where a suitable location would be found to establish a summer camp as a base of operations for the remainder of the campaigning season and from where Varus himself would receive delegations from the local tribes, those already well disposed towards Rome and those who lay ready to be persuaded of the rectitude of such a position.

The exact time of Varus' departure from Vetera is unclear, but we know that in the Roman calendar, the year began with the onset of the campaigning season in the month of *Martius* – aptly named after Mars, the god of war and that the season drew to a close in the eighth month, known both then and now as October. It makes perfect sense therefore that Varus' timetable meant that his planned operations in Germania Magna would last no more than five months and that the troops would be back in quarters before the onset of winter.

Setting off a little after sunrise the troops formed up and, stepping off in a prescribed order, approached the narrow pontoon bridge that linked both banks of the Rhine. In accordance with standard procedure, the first unit to cross onto the eastern bank would have been an *ala* of auxiliary cavalry which was tasked with covering the crossing of the vanguard and then, as

the army slowly assembled on the far side of the river, to scout ahead of the main body to give advance warning of any problems that might be encountered. Next came half of the auxiliary infantry, possibly in this instance as many as six cohorts, immediately followed by a detachment drawn from one of the legions to provide direct close support should the forward elements get into trouble. Attached to this part of the column were a number of troops detailed to act as trailblazers cum engineers who would clear the path for the main body of the army and then, at the end of the day's march, mark out the site for the marching camp. Directly behind this advance group marched the colour parties, bearing the three legionary *aquilae*, with Varus and his headquarters staff – almost certainly accompanied by Gaius Numonius Vala and possibly the three legionary legates. Accompanying Varus' personal baggage would also have been a number of heavily guarded wagons each containing a number of heavy, iron-bound chests, the contents of which – several million denarii in coin and bullion – would be used to cover the remainder of the troops' salaries, which were due to be paid out in early May and early September.

Although the disposition of the leading elements of the marching column followed a standard formula, we will undoubtedly never know the exact deployment of the main body. The reason for this being simply that Varus had two options available to him. If we readily accept the proposition that he believed himself that he was marching either through friendly or completely

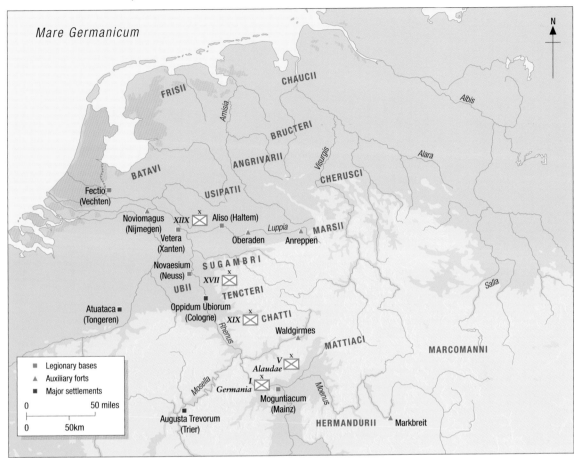

pacified territory, the legions would have followed the headquarters group in turn with each legion being followed by its own baggage train, in which case the rear of the army would have been brought up by the remaining auxiliary cohorts and an *ala* of auxiliary cavalry, with the flanks of the column being screened by the remaining mounted auxiliaries supported by infantry detachments.

This assumption, however, tends to ignore the character and experience of Varus' immediate subordinates. If instead of the initial preposition, we instead accept a second assertion that these were in fact three veteran legions 'An Army unexcelled in bravery, the first of Roman armies in discipline, in energy and in experience in the field' (Paterculus, *History of Rome*, Book ii, Ch. cxix), then the likelihood would have been that, once the troops had crossed the Rhine and were – in the strictest sense – no longer in Roman territory, the column would instead have been deployed *in expedita*. In this version of the marching column, the first two legions followed directly behind the headquarters group, with the third legion being assigned to protect the combined baggage of all three units, the rationale being that the two unencumbered legions would be able to deploy quickly for combat should there be any sudden change in the army's situation.

Although Varus' army was in no way as large as those commanded by his predecessors it still represented a considerable logistical challenge for its

Detail of a Germanic cauldron handle, showing the head of a warrior with his hair dressed in a typical 'Suebian' topknot.

commander to maintain strict control over an unwieldy and extended column. In *The Jewish Revolt*, Josephus suggests that a legion in column of march, with the troops marching six abreast and with a spacing of 3 Roman feet (87cm) between ranks, would occupy 1,524m (1,667 yards), a figure which could reasonably be extended to 1,645m (1,800 yards) if one were to take into account the necessary gaps between the various elements. Complementary to this, John Peddie in *The Roman War Machine* calculates that a single legion on the march would have required some 1,675 pack animals (either led or pulling transport) and that based on the premise that these animals or carts would be deployed two abreast the legion train would be 3,315m (3,625 yards) long. This would mean that *legiones XVII, XIIX* and *XIX* alone would cover some 15km (9 miles) and if we were to consider the various auxiliary units present with the army as being themselves the combined equivalent of a legion, the total column would have been between 19 and 21km (12 and 13 miles) in length.

Whilst in the field, the troops soon fell into a standard marching routine. Commencing at daybreak, the force would march for several hours, covering an average distance of 26km (16 miles) before the trailblazers halted and began marking out the boundaries and principal fixtures of the new marching camp and, under the gaze of the cavalry scouts, as the troops began to file into the encampment they were assigned to the construction work. If the army was deemed to be in hostile terrain, the lead formation would immediately form up for combat in order to deter enemy attack, whilst the succeeding units in the column would begin setting up the camp itself. This meant that the advance units would be in the new day's camp almost before the rearguard had left the previous day's, and in order to compensate for this the units of the main body were rotated sequentially, with each legion being detailed in turn to the baggage train. On every third or fourth day the whole army would rest and remain in camp whilst scouts were sent out to reconnoitre the terrain ahead, thus – in normal circumstances – the column could be expected to cover an average of 135km (84 miles) per week.

Marching along the valley of the Lippe and still relatively fresh, the troops first arrived at the site of the earlier marching camp at Holsterhausen, some 32km (20 miles) east of Vetera, where the existing defensive trace was undoubtedly used as a template for the overnight encampment. From here, a further day's march found the column at Aliso, the main Roman base on the Lippe built on a line of hills overlooking the river. To the east of the camp a second base had been built directly onto the river bank, protected on its remaining three sides by a ditched and embanked rampart, the whole encompassing a number of covered slipways and sheds serving as an advance station of the Rhine fleet.

As the column had by now entered the territory of the Sugambri and the Usipatii, two tribes with a lengthy anti-Roman history, Varus decided to extend the army's rest period at Aliso by a few days in order to await additional reports from his forward scouts, and whilst the troops rested he used the time available to hold a number of planning meetings both with his immediate subordinates and with the officers in charge of providing naval support to the advancing troops. As the initial phase of the march to the Weser would be along the Lippe, many of Varus' logistical problems would have been somewhat eased, but, despite this, the fact is that his relatively small army would still have required almost 40 tons of grain, fodder and other supplies per day. As such these supplies needed to be readily stockpiled and – if both possible and practicable – carried to the other bases further along the river in order that they would not only be waiting for Varus as he advanced along the valley, but also that there would be a suitable reserve already established at the final encampment in the chain of fortifications, thus giving him the full use of his baggage train to move the supplies the relatively short distance from the Lippe to his planned summer camp. During these meetings, and regardless of his own plans, Arminius would have simply played the part of a conscientious cavalry officer, reporting accurately and succinctly when required. Here, so close to the areas of Roman influence, he needed to reaffirm his bona fides to such a degree that when the army finally left the protection of the river and struck inland towards the Weser, his would be an opinion to which Varus would pay attention.

After perhaps a week's sojourn at Aliso, and satisfied about his arrangements, Varus now gave instructions for the column to continue on its march, this time following the course of the Lippe in a south-easterly direction towards the camp at Oberaden, some 32km (20 miles) distant. But before leaving the camp – and on the assumption that this important outpost is synonymous with the camp at Aliso the existence of which is attested by authors such as Dio, Paterculus and Syme – he also appointed Lucius Caedicius, the veteran 50-year-old *praefectus castrorum* (camp prefect) of *legio XIX* as garrison commander, with a force of possibly two cohorts. This command, we must assume, being augmented by one or two units of auxiliary troops already *in situ*.

Following the Lippe as it gently meandered through its valley, the Romans continued east, the pace of the troops being matched by the cargo vessels plying their route between Aliso and the various encampments along the way, each of them being put into a reputable state of defence and garrisoned by units detached from the column, past Beckinghausen and Oberaden on the southern bank of the river before eventually reaching Anreppen, roughly 16km (10 miles) from the source of the Lippe and perhaps the last link in a chain of Roman fortifications stretching back over

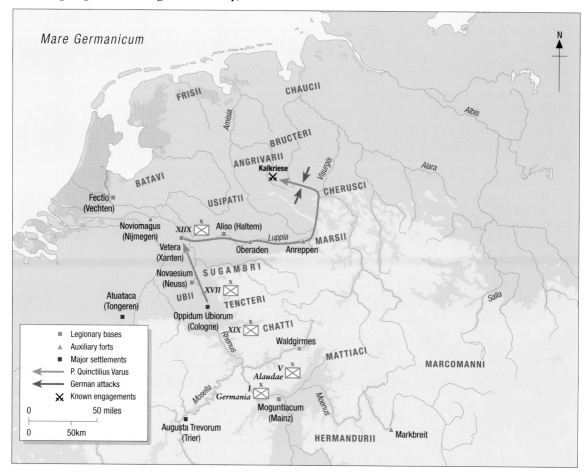

160km (100 miles) to the *hiberna* along the Rhine. Here, Varus decided to establish his forward supply base where waterborne cargoes from Aliso and the ports along the Rhine could be unloaded and stored before being freighted forwards to the summer camp on the Weser. Again, Varus undoubtedly rested his troops for several days before setting off on the next leg of his journey, the march into *Barbaricum* proper, probably not leaving Anreppen before the beginning of April.

The plan was that Varus would continue to the site of his summer camp, and, with his base of operations secure, use the remaining months of the campaigning season to support the various pro-Roman chieftains by underlining Roman superiority, both culturally and militarily, before breaking camp in early August and retracing his steps westwards along the Lippe, collecting the garrisons from those temporary outposts scheduled to be abandoned, while at the same time reinforcing and resupplying those forts that would be occupied over the winter months until their relief the following spring. Forming up into their well-practised formations and almost certainly led by Arminius' auxiliaries who were, after all, now in their home territory, the troops struck northwards towards the Visurgis, the river Weser, leaving a reinforced garrison – possibly similar in size to that which had been left at Aliso – to guard the base and help to maintain the increasingly tenuous lines of communication.

Although the force that Varus led from the camp at Anreppen had by now been reduced to about 21 cohorts of legionaries, six of auxiliary infantry and three *alae* of auxiliary cavalry, he still had some 13,500 effectives under arms. It was a force that, in normal circumstances, could be considered as being more than sufficient to overawe the natives for the remainder of the summer season before the return journey to Vetera.

For over a week the column snaked northwards, strung out along the tracks that were a far cry from the military roads the soldiers were used to until Arminius, riding at the front of the column, sent a rider back to the advance guard announcing that he had reached the prospective campsite. Virtually nothing is known that will positively identify the location of Varus' summer camp – recent excavations at Barkhausen had initially led archaeologists to believe that they had discovered the site, but given the lack of an architectural trace such as that found at Aliso or Anreppen there is little evidence of the existence of fixed defences. Thus the actual location of Varus' camp may actually lie somewhere under the streets of Minden, some kilometres further to the north of Barkhausen.

Given that Arminius' loyalty was as yet unquestioned, and that Cheruscan territory was viewed as a friendly environment, the normal procedure of deploying the cavalry and a significant portion of the infantry as a defensive measure was set aside and the troops were set to work following a long-established timetable so that, as Varus and his party came up, the army's summer camp had already begun to take shape. Firstly, the *praetorium*, the headquarters area, was pegged out, followed by the position of the four main gates (the *portae praetoria, decumana, principalis dextra* and *principalis sinistra*) and then the main internal roads which quartered the interior of the camp, each being named after the gate at which it terminated. Of the main defences, the first to be constructed was an exterior ditch or *fosse*, the spill from which was then used to construct an earth rampart or *agger* faced with turf sod, this last being surmounted by a wooden palisade. Once their section of the defences had been constructed, the troops would march to their allotted area of the camp and pitch their tents. (In adverse weather conditions, this order would have been reversed so that the tents would have been pitched first in order that the troops would be provided with adequate dry shelter.) With the bulk of the troops now present, the four towered gates would now be completed and a number of troops detailed to construct the storage areas. Finally, and to facilitate the interior movement of troops around the defences, a fifth internal road – the *via sagularis* – was built around the interior circuit of the defensive palisade.

SUMMER MANOEUVRES

Given that we are able to deduce Varus' movements to and from his summer camp with some degree of accuracy, it is clear that this forward base was occupied for a little over four months. So one question that must be asked is what did he do during this time, before making the fateful decision to divert his forces and return to the Rhine by an alternative route?

Three of the Roman authors – Marcus Velleius Paterculus, Lucius Annaeus Florus and Cassius Dio – are quite explicit in their opinion that Varus threw caution to the wind, preferring the mailed fist to the velvet glove.

Chronologically the first of the trio, Paterculus (*History of Rome*, Book II, Ch. cxvii) writes:

When placed in charge of the army of Germany, he entertained the notion that the Germans were a people who were men only in limbs and voice, and that they, who could not be subdued by the sword, could be soothed by the law. With this purpose in mind he entered the heart of Germany as though he were going through a people enjoying the blessings of peace, and sitting on his tribunal he wasted the time of a summer campaign in holding court and observing the proper details of legal procedure.

Writing in the 2nd century AD, Florus (*The Epitome of Roman History*, Book II, Ch. xxx) continues in a similar vein:

But it is more difficult to retain than to create provinces; they are won by force, they are secured by justice. Therefore our joy was short-lived; for the Germans had been defeated rather than subdued, and under the rule of Drusus they respected our moral qualities rather than our arms. After his death they began to detest the licentiousness and pride not less than the cruelty of Quintillius

Tombstone of Marcus Caelius, centurion *legio XIIX*. Erected by Caelius' brother, who was himself a career soldier. The inscription reads: 'To Marcus Caelius, son of Titus, of the Lemonian Tribe, from Bologna. First Centurion of the XIIX Legion. Aged 53, he was killed in the Varian War. Should his bones be found, let them be interred here. Publius Caelius, son of Titus, of the Lemonian Tribe, erected this.'
On the tombstone, we see an image of Caelius carrying his vine staff of office, the *paludamentum* cloak of a senior officer and full military decorations including an oak leaf *corona civica*, which was awarded for saving the life of a fellow citizen in battle. Flanking Caelius are two of his manumitted slaves who, it must be assumed, also lost their lives in the battle.

Varus. He had the temerity to hold an assembly and had issued an edict against the Catthi, just as though he could restrain the violence of barbarians by the rod of a lictor and the proclamation of a herald.

(By referring to 'Quintillius Varus' and the 'Catthi', Florus obviously means 'Quinctilius Varus' and the 'Chatti' respectively).

Finally, Dio (*The Roman History: the Reign of Augustus*, Book 56, Ch. 18) remarks that 'when Quinctilius Varus became governor of the province of Germany, and in the exercise of his powers also came to handle the affairs of these peoples, he tried to hasten and to widen the process of change. He not only gave orders to the Germans as if they were actual slaves of the Romans, but also levied money from them as if they were subject nations.'

If we accept these three quotes at face value, it would seem obvious to the most impartial reader that Varus was in fact the architect of his own destruction. However it is also certain that both Florus and Dio would most likely have borrowed heavily from Paterculus and thus it is easy to understand why his particular bias pervades these later works. A fourth source, used by Tacitus as a reference for his *Germania*, is Pliny the Elder's *History of the German Wars*. This history, which may have included material relative to Varus' tenure in Germany, has regrettably been lost to us and thus we have no real contemporary source to measure or compare Paterculus against.

Modern critics have pointed out Paterculus' overt praise of his former commander who was, after all, emperor when the *History of Rome* was published, but there is a darker shadow to the work which must also be considered. Paterculus is known to have been a close associate of Lucius Aelius Sejanus, Tiberius' highly ambitious prefect of the Praetorian Guard who, in AD 26, had Varus' wife Claudia Pulchra executed on a dubious charge of treason and then the following year wiped out his direct line with the arraignment and death of his son and heir, Publius Quinctilius Varus filius, under similar circumstances. It may therefore be that Paterculus was not as

In the grounds surrounding the museum, this metal relief map gives a graphic depiction of the Weg der Römer, the route of the legionaries' final march. Geographical 'north' is in the upper left-hand corner of the plate.

TOP

On the Weg der Römer, this iron plate commemorates the initial finds, in 1989, of artefacts that had lain where they had fallen for almost two millennia.

BOTTOM

Steel plate marking the site of the find, in 1994, of the first human remains on the battlefield. Sometime after the battle, these remains had been re-interred with a number of animal bones, which may have indicated some form of Germanic rite or the reburial of what were believed to be the skeletons of Varus' troops by Germanicus' army when he came across the battlefield some years later.

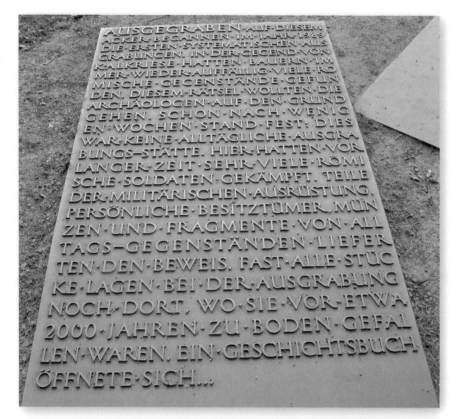

unbiased an observer as has been normally assumed and that he had deliberately blackened Varus' reputation because of his friendship with Sejanus who was at that time, after the Emperor Tiberius, undoubtedly the most powerful man in Rome. A clarification of this attitude might possibly have been found in the planned expansion to his *History of Rome* to which he often alludes, but the author himself disappears from the pages of history shortly after AD 31, when he was presumably implicated in Sejanus' plot to overthrow Tiberius and seize power for himself.

For the troops, much of the time spent at the summer encampment would have been no different from any other station in the empire and, if we temporarily suspend judgement on Varus' own actions, it is certain that, apart from the occasions when a military presence was required at a location in order to reinforce Rome's prestige, much of the time would have been spent either drilling the troops or embarking on a number of civil engineering projects. Although we have no record that Varus had spent any of the previous summers in Germania Magna, it would be reasonable to assume that the site of the *castrum aestivum* of AD 9 was actually intended as an extension of the line of outposts along the Lippe Valley, effectively pushing outwards the area reachable by Roman troops, and that therefore the route back to the river would have needed to have been improved, not only from the aspect of better communication with the Rhine bases, and thence to Rome, but also with regard to the simple logistics of bringing forwards the supplies stockpiled at Anreppen.

TO DIVIDE AND RULE

Perhaps the most crucial aspect of Varus' governorship in Syria had been his ability to maintain the peace whilst simultaneously dealing with the numerous secular and religious groupings and this had been the fundamental reason for his appointment to the command of the German military district.

In almost all of her dealings with foreign powers, Rome invariably followed a policy known as *divide et impera* – divide and rule – where local factionalism was exploited in order not only to provide opportunities for intervention should they be needed, but also to create a friendly power base to support Roman interests. If Varus were to lay the foundations of a future Roman province of Germania Magna, then he would need to find allies to support and promote Roman interests. The obvious question to be answered was who would these allies be and where would they be found?

Many of the German tribes – the Sugambri and the Suebii, for example – were inveterately hostile to Rome, whilst others such as the Chatti had shown themselves to be rather flexible in their concept of loyalty having fought, on occasion, both for and against Rome. Alternatively both the Frisii and the Ubii could be counted upon, and had most likely provided a number of auxiliary units for service in Varus' army, but neither tribe had any presence east of the Rhine and thus the chances of their being able to influence the tribes on Rome's behalf would have been negligible to say the least. What was needed was someone with a significant following in Germania Magna itself, someone who could be counted upon to speak for Rome in the native councils and gatherings. It must, therefore, have seemed like divine providence when an unknown bureaucrat, noticing Arminius' service record, had suggested that his unit be attached to Varus' command. It was a decision that goes far indeed not only in explaining the choice of Cheruscan territory for the site of the army's summer camp, but also Varus' continued trust of his subordinate in the face of Segestes' allegations. After all, Arminius may have been born into the Cheruscan nobility, but by education and training he was the embodiment of a Roman soldier.

With his transfer to the Army of Germania Inferior, it must have seemed to Arminius that *his* gods were in fact smiling upon him. With his proximity to the Roman high command, he was not only privy to Varus' plans but the

This view of the forest floor, riven by gullies and rivulets shows how treacherous the terrain could be under normal weather conditions. After heavy rainfall and churned by thousands of pairs of heavy marching sandals it would have been rendered into a glutinous mass that would have hindered both combatant armies

longer the army remained in the field he would become increasingly more indispensible to his enemy. Having been educated in Rome, he would no doubt have been aware of the epigram: '*Quem deus veult perdere, dementat prius*' – 'Those whom the gods would destroy, they first make mad', for in nursing this metaphorical viper to his bosom, and ignoring all warnings about his loyalty Varus had ultimately sown the seeds of his own destruction and that of his army.

Throughout the summer, in his dual role as Roman officer and Germanic chieftain, Arminius used his autonomy to forward and perfect his plans, consolidating local support whilst simultaneously seeking allies amongst the other tribes, inciting those who needed no excuse to rise against Rome and skilfully wooing those whose loyalties were all the more ambivalent. In this he was no doubt unwittingly aided by Varus himself for when he entertained the tribal nobility at his headquarters, they saw not a superior culture, but rather an alien one, and then when Varus was invited to arbitrate in a number of carefully orchestrated tribal disputes and offer a 'Roman' judgment it was equally distant from anything anticipated by the plaintiffs. Indeed, this is perhaps what Paterculus might have meant when he described Varus' preoccupation with legal procedure. It was, however, all grist to the mill as far as Arminius was concerned for with each dinner and with each courtroom decision he was able to push his plans further, playing upon growing tribal dissatisfaction to increase his influence.

As the months wore on, and by now apparently lulled into a sense of false security, Varus continued to pursue the agenda of a politician rather than that of military commander. But it was for Arminius that the sands of time were running out and as June passed into July he needed quickly to devise a method by which his enemy could be induced not only to delay his departure for the

Rhine, but also to change the axis of his return entirely onto a route specifically chosen for him. Accordingly, Arminius arranged for some of his allies – either the Angrivarii or the Bructeri – to launch a series of raids into Cheruscan territory and then when news of these attacks reached the Roman encampment advised Varus that if he wanted to show the tribes the benefit of closer ties with Rome the best way to do so would be to send troops into the affected areas in order to deter further raids. That Varus did in fact accede to Arminius' request is supported by Dio (Book 56, Ch. 19) who, albeit with the benefit of hindsight in which he refers to Germania Magna as 'hostile', states that 'consequently he did not keep his legions together, as was proper in a hostile country, but distributed many of the soldiers to helpless communities, which asked for them for the alleged purpose of guarding various points, arresting robbers, or escorting provision trains'. Despite the presence of Roman troops the unrest continued, and over the following weeks patrols and work parties were also attacked – undoubtedly not only by the tribesmen, but also by the men of Arminius' own cavalry *ala* who, equipped as Roman troops, would have been able to get close to their targets and strike before any alarm could be raised. Although only isolated pinpricks, the increasing number of attacks should have placed Varus on his guard and persuaded him to take suitable countermeasures, but gulled by his trusted lieutenant he did nothing.

Even as it seemed that Arminius had achieved his principal objectives, his plans almost unravelled when his father-in-law, a chieftain named Segestes, denounced him and his confederates to Varus, privately warning the legate of the plan to attack the column on its return to the Rhine. One reason for the intense animosity between the two men apparently lay in the fact that Segestes' daughter Thusnelda had previously eloped with Arminius and married him against her father's wishes. As Tacitus (*Annals of Imperial Rome*,

Fallen trees were not the only obstacles that the Roman column had to negotiate in their march westwards. Even a minor detour to avoid a forest pool such as this one would have cost them precious time, time that – ultimately – the legionaries didn't have.

BETRAYAL (pp. 46–47)

With the main summer camp established near Minden, numerous detachments of troops were sent out both on patrol or to conduct engineering work – such as road construction – and as such were the perfect target for enemy ambush. Here we see a unit of legionaries having encountered a patrol of Cheruscan auxiliary cavalry whilst they are themselves engaged in repairing a ford across a stream. Their guard down, the Romans assume nothing untoward and the two bodies of troops mingle, and the majority of the infantrymen continue with their labours, whilst the two commanding officers converse with each other.

As a prearranged signal, the Cheruscan officer draws his long-bladed cavalry sword (*spatha*) and viciously strikes down the centurion in charge of the work detail **(1)**. With all pretence cast aside, the Cheruscans now begin to attack their erstwhile allies

(2). Although army regulations insist that the legionaries wear their personal weapons (i.e. sword and dagger) whilst working **(3)**, many of the men are simply too shocked at the auxiliaries' actions and fail to defend themselves, being cut down where they stand. Others, unable to reach their stacked arms **(4)** attempt, instead, to flee for the dubious safety of the forest and are ridden down by the vengeful German horsemen **(5)** whose orders are to leave no survivors who can bring word of Arminius' treachery back to Varus.

In various incarnations, this scene was played out on numerous occasions during the summer months, the losses – although minimal – serving only to provoke Varus into amending his plans and converting what should have been an easy return journey back to the winter camps on the Rhine into a punitive expedition against both the Angrivarii and the Bructeri.

Book 1, Ch. 58) in his description of the later capture of Segestes by Germanicus in AD 15 writes:

> From the moment when the deified Augustus made me a Roman citizen I have chosen my friends and my enemies with a view to your interests: not from hatred of my own country (for the traitor is loathsome even to the party of his choice), but because I took the advantage of Rome and Germany to be one, and peace a better thing than war. For that reason I accused Arminius – to me the abductor of a daughter, to you the violator of a treaty – in presence of Varus, then at the head of your army.

The speaker's pro-Roman stance seems to shine through Tacitus' prose, but if he were so convinced of where his people's best interests lay, the question that must be asked is why did he delay in bringing his concerns to Varus?

In order to conceal the source of this potentially explosive intelligence, Segestes then asked Varus 'to lay in irons Arminius, his accomplices, and myself', but the Roman demurred and decided against challenging his subordinate, an undoubted factor in Segestes' future survival following Arminius' triumph. In any event there was little opportunity for him to press his case further as news was now received that the unrest was escalating, with Arminius plausibly arguing that the revolt needed to be nipped in the bud before the discontent could spread to other tribes. A counter argument was then raised to the effect that it was too late in the campaigning season for the army to mount operations against the rebels and return to its winter stations before the weather broke. But then, just as it seemed as if he had lost his gamble, Arminius carefully baited the trap. It would be possible for the army to both chastise the insurgents *and* reach the Rhine before the onset of winter if it marched westwards not via the Lippe as intended, but by an alternative route leading through the lands of the Angrivarii themselves, a route which was markedly shorter than that originally planned. He would also, of course, muster the Cheruscan warriors and lead them against the enemy. As Dio (Ch 56, Book 19) writes 'Then there came an uprising, first on the part of those who lived at a distance from him, deliberately so arranged, in order that Varus should march against them and so be more easily overpowered while proceeding through what was supposed to be friendly country.'

(It should of course be noted that here, Dio once again implies that Germany has been pacified and is 'friendly', a statement that is at odds with his earlier comments within the same chapter regarding the disposition of Varus' forces against the tribal raids.)

For a few moments the silence was undoubtedly palpable as Varus carefully weighed his options and then sought the opinions of his legates and senior officers. Perhaps the tedium of the summer had been excessive, but the thought of imminent action against one of the lesser Germanic tribes was too enticing and a consensus was soon reached that Arminius was right and that the veteran legions could easily chastise the tribesmen before sweeping them aside and pushing on to the Rhine.

With the fateful decision thus made, orders were given to bring up additional stores from Anreppen as the army would, initially at least, be operating on an overextended line of supply and would need to carry as much *matériel* as possible in order to support the troops firstly in the inevitable combat with the Angrivarii and then having achieved the breakthrough until a suitable forward supply line could be established with the base at Vetera.

THE TROOPS MOVE OUT, 7 SEPTEMBER

During the morning of 7 September, Varus ordered the camp to be struck and, as the troops completed their allotted tasks, they assembled in their units in review order. On this day, however, it was not a normal parade as the troops were to receive the third instalment of the *stipendium*, their annual salary, and as a result the regimental coffers were soon awash with coin as soldiers cleared debts and deposited funds with their units' savings clubs. Almost two millennia later, many of these lost coins would lead to the excavation of the Kalkriese site.

When all was ready and the campsite cleared, pickets were set and the remainder of the army stood to attention as Varus mounted the tribunal to address the troops. He told them of the change in plans, that instead of marching back to the Lippe and thence to the Rhine they would be marching to war, marching against the tribesmen who had been responsible for the deaths of a number of their comrades. Attempting to allay any misapprehension on the part of the troops he sought to reassure them that the new route was shorter than that originally planned, adding that when the enemy had been crushed the army would be permitted to loot their settlements. As the inevitable cheers died down, a trumpet call sounded and preceded by a screen of cavalry the army began slowly to move off in the 'approach to battle' or '*in exercita*' with two legions in the van and the third bringing up the rear, guarding the army's combined baggage, the whole screened by the auxiliary infantry.

Setting off later than usual, the army continued its march through relatively open country, halting in mid-afternoon, still having covered the obligatory daily total of 26km (16 miles) and, as preparations were made for the army to encamp for the evening, Arminius took his leave of Varus,

As part of a museum exhibition at Kalkriese entitled *Feldzeichen zum Friedenzeichen*, a number of local inhabitants of foreign extraction were invited to decorate a stylized Roman standard with a message of peace in their native language. Here we see examples from Germany, Greece, France, Cyprus, Denmark and several other countries.

ostensibly to complete the Cheruscan muster. Mounting his horse, he promised that the lighter-armed warriors would catch up with the slower-moving legionaries within the following two to three days. It would be the last time that the two men ever met. Before departing, however, he cleverly left a select number of his men with the column, officially to serve Varus as guides but in reality to enable him to keep a close watch on the Roman column and amend his plans as necessary. It was an astute move as, with Segestes' warnings now forgotten, no one in the Roman high command could conceive of any ulterior motive on Arminius' part. And yet, with his departure the number of mounted troops with the army dropped by over a quarter, thus reducing Varus' own ability to conduct a forward reconnaissance and maintain the obligatory flank and rear protection for the marching column, effectively making him more dependent upon Arminius' men. As the rearmost elements of Varus' army began to arrive in the new encampment, their erstwhile ally was riding furiously north-west to confer with his allies of the Angrivarii and Bructeri.

THE ANABASIS, 8 SEPTEMBER

The next morning, and following long-established routine, the army broke camp at daybreak preparatory to beginning the day's march at 7am. Again, the troops moved off prepared for battle, but after a few miles the path that they were following entered an area of heavy forest and accordingly the rate of march slowed considerably with both men and transport unable to maintain the regulation formation distances. Thus the army became strung out, not only critically extending the distance between the van and rearguard elements, but also compromising Varus' own ability to maintain control over his forces.

This standard was dedicated as part of the *Feldzeichen zum Friedenszeichen* exhibition by the German Chancellor Dr Angela Merkel.

After his departure from the column the previous evening, Arminius had put the final stages together in the gathering of the Cheruscan host, which would indeed catch up with the Roman column as he had promised, but without the anticipated intentions. With Varus marching on the route chosen for him, it simply remained for the tribes to ensure that he remained committed to that route, unable to reverse his direction and push southwards to the relative security of Anreppen and the Lippe Valley where, even if the army were to become surrounded or besieged, he would at least have restored riverine communications with the Rhine forts.

Accordingly, the more numerous Bructeri were to launch a number of spoiling attacks on the legionaries, whilst the Angrivarii were to prepare an ambush site near Kalkriese where the path that the Romans were following entered into an area of thick forest before debouching into a narrow defile sandwiched between an area of hills to the south and a large area of bogland to the north.

At some time during the late morning, the Bructeri launched the first of a number of hit-and-run attacks against the length of the column, forcing the troops to halt and change direction as required, the adverse terrain preventing them from maintaining the solid battle line which was their greatest advantage over a tribal enemy. Hitting the Romans from all sides, these

Taken from the viewing platform on the top of the museum, this westward-looking perspective shows the final battlefield. Although the lower slopes of the Kalkrieser Berg to the left of the image would have been forested, the wooded area to the right of the picture would have been flat bogland and, as such, difficult going for the retreating legionaries.

attacks did not, however, consist of the showers of spears and javelins launched from a distance that are described by many authors. Quite simply, for many of the Germans, these would be their only weapons apart from a cudgel or a knife and there were no massive stockpiles available from which to replace them. The warriors' aim at this early stage in the battle was simply to tire the enemy and cause as much material damage as possible before pulling back and regrouping to prepare for another attack. It was a perfect strategy for if the legionaries were tired, then their reactions would be slower and possibly give the tribesmen a crucial opening that could be exploited. In addition to this whilst a fatality simply meant one less soldier in the enemy column, an increasing number of wounded would gradually place a heavy strain upon the baggage train, and eventually onto the legions themselves as increasing numbers of able-bodied fighting men were withdrawn from the fighting line in order to care for the casualties.

As the Bructeri withdrew, possibly accompanied by Arminius' guides who had served their purpose by ensuring that the enemy walked into the trap, the column pushed ever onwards through the forest maze, nervously awaiting further attacks. The next trial for the Romans however, came not from flanks or rear, but rather from above as a sudden torrential downpour turned the forest path into a quagmire, reducing their rate of march to a veritable crawl as the advancing troops had to contend with increasingly adverse terrain. Eventually, the beleaguered legionaries broke out into open ground and, unable to proceed further in the heavy rain, the order was given to make camp.

Despite the shock of the running ambush and the steadily deteriorating weather, the marching camp was built in relatively good order. With one of the leading legions 'stood to' in battle formation in order to repel any potential enemy attacks, whilst the succeeding troops actually began the construction of the stockade itself. A crucial point to note here is that in adverse weather conditions, the first task for each unit was not in fact to begin work on the defensive trace, but rather to pitch its tents in order that the men would have shelter from the elements. The reason that this consideration is important is that a number of modern commentators suggest that, as a result of the heavy rainfall, the legionaries' shields had become waterlogged and were at this stage too heavy for them to be used effectively in combat. There are two factors, however, that would seem to bring this hypothesis into question. The first is that in order to deliberately build up their endurance and stamina, the legionaries' training equipment was twice as heavy as the normal issue. Secondly, the legionaries' shield covers were made from waxed goat leather, which was in fact the same material from which their highly waterproof tents were constructed and would thus have displayed similar characteristics. It would therefore seem to indicate that water repellancy of the covers was not as decisive a factor in the running battle as has previously been believed.

That evening, as sentries huddled in their cloaks peering out through the rainfall on the alert for enemy activity, Varus held a council of war in his headquarters tent. Voices were muted as each of the legates was asked to present his unit returns, followed in turn by the auxiliary officers. Overall, casualties suffered by the column had been relatively light, helped firstly by the fact that the tribesmen had seemed unwilling to press home their attacks and secondly by the heavy rainfall which had adversely affected the movement of both sides – The Romans' inability to pursue their attackers being negated by the Germans' inability to escape if cornered. An area of concern was then raised, namely the vulnerability of both the auxiliary cavalry and the baggage train whilst moving through the thick woods. In the case of the former, the combination of horse and rider made a far easier target for the enemy marksmen, and the sudden flight of a panicked and wounded horse could

Unlike the easily recognizable *pila*, these leaf-shaped javelin heads could have been used by either Roman auxiliary troops or their Germanic opponents. (AKG Images/Varusschlacht Museum, Kalkriese)

DEATH IN THE FOREST (pp. 54–55)

Over the course of three days, the fatal combination of harassing attacks by both the Angrivarii and the Bructeri, together with the adverse terrain and inclement weather has meant that the legions have been unable to maintain their usual march integrity. Strung out along the forest paths, units **(1)** have now devolved into small groups of men all of whom are simply pushing forwards in an attempt to reach the relative safety of the next marching camp.

Here, one centurion **(2)**, having been attacked by a number of Bructeri warriors, has killed or wounded two of his opponents whilst attempting to shield the remainder of his unit who are following as best they can. Unlike centurions of the Caesarian period, who were to wear their military decorations at all times, this officer wears a simple mail shirt, much like the rest of his men and is really distinguished only by the transverse crest on his helmet, his silvered greaves and the fact that his personal

weapons are worn on the opposite side of the body to those of the rank and file (i.e. the *gladius* is worn on the left). Immediately to his rear are two legionaries **(3)**, one of whom is badly wounded, and is being supported by his comrade rather than being left to make his own way through the carnage.

Having ambushed the column, the Bructeri are trying to attack stragglers or small, unformed groups. Of the six warriors engaged, the majority of them are normal levies **(4)**, which make up the greater part of the attacking force, whilst the remaining two are clearly members of the noble caste **(5)**, as demonstrated by the quality of their clothing, arms and equipment. The bearded warrior, shown drawing his sword, is wearing both a mail shirt and an auxiliary-style helmet, which may indicate previous service in the Roman army or may simply be the spoils of war **(6)**.

create havoc in the tightly packed ranks as they plodded along the forest paths. Measures of varying severity could be taken to alleviate this, including even the abandonment of the horses, but the main problem lay with the baggage train. Its presence not only dictated how the army progressed on the march, but both the drovers and wagon drivers were noncombatants and thus, if the enemy were to break through the flank guards, the potential for critical damage to the army's ability to function was enormous.

The meeting continued for a number of hours with opinions being offered about the column's tactical position. Many present felt – quite rightly – that the day's fighting had simply been intended to keep the troops off balance, and that when Arminius and his Cheruscans arrived they would be able to take the fight to the enemy. Some officers however, asked what had happened to Arminius' scouts, believing that they may have been cut off from the main body or killed. The unasked question of whether they had been involved in the day's ambushes remained tantalizingly unanswered. As the meeting drew to a close, Varus gave his instructions for the following day – if the heavy rainfall did not abate the army would remain in camp whilst scouting parties were sent out to probe the route ahead.

MUDBOUND, 9 SEPTEMBER

As feared, the downpour continued with the luckier amongst the troops remaining within the limited shelter of their tents whilst their comrades manned the defences, scanning the horizon for any sign of moving troops. Just before the sun rose, a small group of mounted men slipped out of the *porta decumana*, the rearward-facing gate with orders to retrace the army's steps until they met Arminius and the Cheruscan host. Once they had met up with the auxiliary prefect, they were to apprise him of the army's situation and urge him to make all speed to catch up with Varus and his troops, which would allow the army to take the offensive and regain the tactical initiative. Shortly afterwards, a second body of men left the encampment, this time by the main gate, their orders were to scout the terrain ahead and, if possible, locate the enemy, ascertaining their strength and position. Above all they were to ensure that the path ahead was practicable enough for the army to continue its onward march.

After several hours the scouting party returned to the camp. They had been unable to find any trace of the enemy, but reported that the storm had in places turned the forest track into a sea of glutinous mud that would be hard enough going for the infantry and cavalry, but almost impassable to wheeled transport. In addition to this they had noted a number of sites where trees had fallen across the path and would need to be cleared away before the main body would be able to pass.

Meanwhile, and unseen by Varus or any of his officers, Arminius' duplicity had already fatally manifested itself. Those riders who had earlier left the camp under cover of darkness had been surprised to find him several kilometres closer to the laager than had been anticipated, and with great relief rode into the centre of his encampment in order to deliver their dispatches, believing that the army would soon be extricated from its precarious position. But instead of meeting the anticipated friendly reception, they were seized almost as soon as they had dismounted and roughly dragged before the Cheruscan leader.

GERMANS
A Angrivarii
B Bructeri
C Cherusci

ROMANS
1 Roman encampment
2 Numonius Vala
3 Lucius Eggius

KALKRIESER BERG

EVENTS

Afternoon, 10 September

1 Varus sends Numonius Vala at the head of the best
remaining cavalry to skirt the enemy positions and ride
towards the Rhine in order to warn the garrisons of the
army's defeat.

2 Vala's force is attacked by a flanking force of mixed
Cheruscan cavalry and infantry and is destroyed.

Evening, 10 September

3 Varus and his senior officers commit suicide. Joint
command devolves upon the camp prefects of *legiones
XVII* and *XIIX* – Lucius Eggius and Caeonius.

Morning, 11 September

4 Lucius Eggius leads the remainder of his legion,
augmented by survivors of *legio XIX*, in a further
advance, to be followed by Caeonius and the remainder
of the army.

5 The Bructeri launch a number of limited, harassing
attacks on the Roman column as it passes by the slopes
of the Kalkrieser Berg.

6 A further flanking force of Cheruscan warriors, under
the personal command of Arminius take up an ambush
position on the wooded heights above Eggius' route.

AN ARMY AT BAY
Afternoon, 10 September to morning 11 September

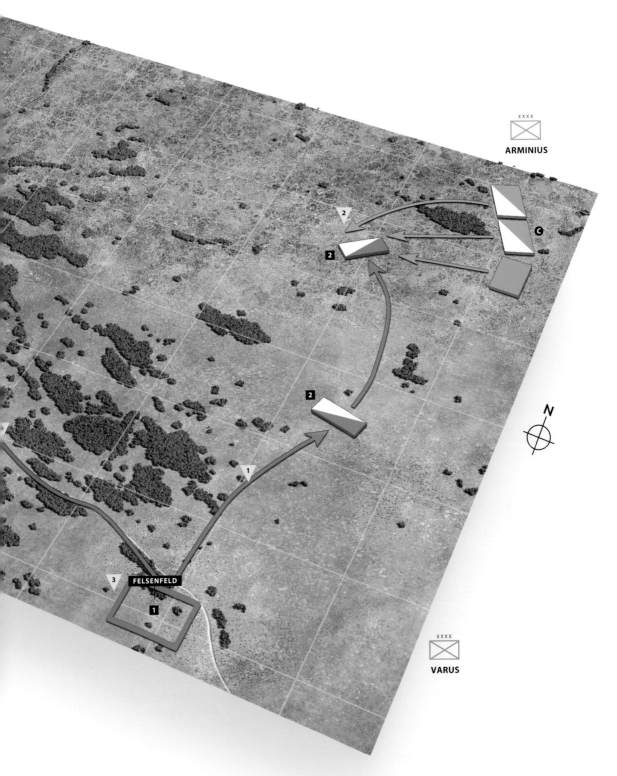

All men have limits to their endurance, and these were men like any other, so after the torture began and before they were finally put to death Arminius had a fairly accurate impression of the state and location of Varus' main body. His plan was working exactly as intended – without local guides, the Romans were marching along a route from which they could not realistically deviate, and thus their every move could be anticipated and planned for. Messengers were sent ahead to both the Angrivarii and Bructeri, ordering them to renew the hit-and-run attacks on the following day and above all to complete the preparation of the ambush site, work on which had obviously been slowed by the inclement weather. Tokens were then sent to those tribes, such as the Sugambri, who were waiting for Arminius' word that the attack on Varus' column had successfully begun, urging them to attack the Roman forts and camps in their vicinity. Germania Magna would soon be ablaze from end to end.

As daylight turned to dusk, bringing no word from the men sent to find Arminius, Varus' spirits fell. The prefect could not have been so far behind the main body, especially if he had been able to mobilize the Cheruscan warriors as had originally been intended. Lightly armed and with an intimate knowledge of the terrain, they should have made good time despite the bad weather, unless of course, Segestes' earlier allegations had been well founded and Arminius had no intention of linking up with the column. With brutal clarity Varus must by now have realized that he had indeed been betrayed and that the army's position was far more dangerous than the relatively light casualties suffered by the column had hitherto indicated.

Fearing a night attack, the camp now became a hive of frenetic activity as fully half of the army was 'stood to' whilst Varus held another council of war. Gone was any trace of previous indolence on the part of the Roman commander. Time was now of the essence and as the meeting continued those officers in attendance received instructions rather than having their opinion solicited. Quietly explaining his fears reagarding the non-appearance of the Cheruscan auxiliaries, Varus issued his orders.

Irrespective of weather conditions, the army would break camp and continue westwards along the forest path; it was after all, their only real option. Both speed and mobility were the key to success and thus the troops would carry only essential equipment. The army could not afford to be tied to its baggage train, and therefore the majority of the wagons would be wrecked and left behind, their loads, where possible, being packed on mules. This would of course, have the indirect benefit of reducing the length of the marching column by some 3–5km (2–3 miles), a distance that could in fact prove crucial as the inevitable running fight developed. Any stores and equipment not brought with the column would be destroyed in order to deny them to the enemy.

The camp itself would not be struck, with any future encampments built during the retreat being constructed from equipment that would be distributed to the troops from army stores before the march. With stocks of *pila* running low a number of the men may even have been issued with ballista bolts taken from the abandoned artillery for use as makeshift javelins, in addition to which, weapons would undoubtedly have been issued to the teamsters and muleteers – it was certain that the Germans would draw no distinction between combatants and noncombatants and also by giving the men the means to defend themselves, however ineffectually, it would at least theoretically ease the problems faced by the rearguard. Finally, the badly wounded would be left behind with a number of the medical staff. Officially this was in the hope of avoiding causing them further suffering, but in reality

– as everyone knew – it was to remove yet another impediment to the army's mobility, sacrificing the few so that the many could live to fight another day.

Around the campfires weapons were being sharpened, final checks and repairs made to personal equipment and, inevitably, amongst members of the individual *contubernia*, the small tactical elements that made up each century, promises given amongst the messmates not to abandon each other on the march, to do what was necessary to ensure that the wounded did not fall alive into enemy hands – their fear of torture or dismemberment in barbarian rites in many cases being greater than any fear that they might have had of dying in battle. Amongst the teamsters, those wagons which were to remain with the column were being checked for damage before being reloaded, their axles being greased to prevent noise, whilst elsewhere the muleteers began to muffle their charges' harness, being careful to wad the bell clappers with strips of cloth or clumps of grass in order to prevent the enemy from getting any accidental warning of the army's departure.

THE VIA DOLOROSA, 10 SEPTEMBER

Before daybreak on 10 September, and without any of the usual trumpet calls or signals which would have normally called the troops to stand to, centurions and junior officers began to rouse their men for the day's march, which would begin without warning the enemy that the army was about to break camp. Having finally convinced himself of Arminius' treachery, Varus now pinned his hopes on cutting his way through the enemy cordon to the west and breaking out of the forest into more open terrain, which would allow the legions to use their superior training and discipline to best advantage.

Within the camp and led by half of the auxiliary infantry, the army formed up in the *praetentura* – the forward area closest to the enemy – and, in silence, began to file out of the main gate, following the trail westwards. Immediately after the advance guard came the first legion, interspersed with the trailblazers and ready for combat, in turn followed by the second legion and then Varus with the army headquarters. The rear was brought up by the third legion and reduced baggage train, escorted by the remaining auxiliary cohorts. With legionary cavalry helping to provide flank cover, the final units to leave the camp were the remnants of the two auxiliary *alae*, which had been placed under the overall command of Numonius Vala. Given the almost total ineffectiveness of the mounted troops during the previous days' fighting in the woods, Varus had elected to use their mobility, such as it was, to delay any immediate pursuit whilst still being in a position to offer additional protection to the rear of the column.

Plunging into the woodland, the leading elements soon found themselves in difficulty. Splashing their way along the muddied trail, they were forced to stop with ever-increasing regularity and forced to adopt a defensive posture whilst fallen trees or other obstacles were dragged aside from the path in order not to impede the advance. Nevertheless, a gradual progress was made and soon only Vala's horsemen and the badly wounded remained in the deserted camp. As his men formed up by the *porta principalis*, Vala cantered over to the small knot of officers who had elected to remain with the wounded, giving them a soldier's blunt advice that they should not trust in the enemy's mercy and let their men be taken alive. With that, he spurred his mount to the head of the small column and rode out of the camp thankful that he had escaped injury so far.

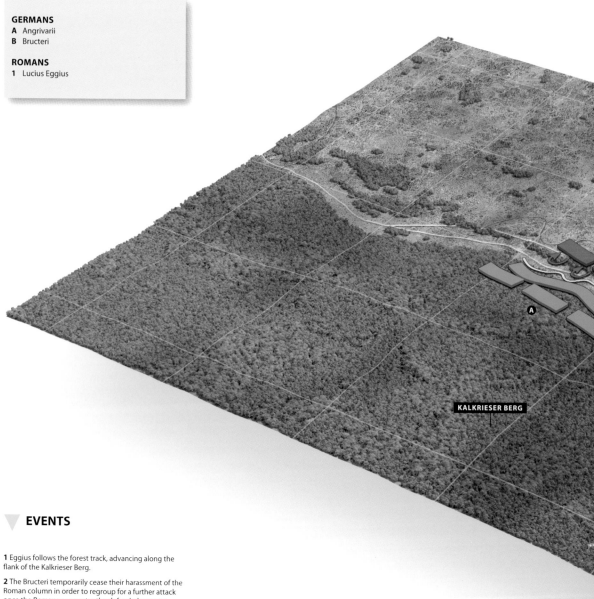

GERMANS
A Angrivarii
B Bructeri

ROMANS
1 Lucius Eggius

KALKRIESER BERG

▼ EVENTS

1 Eggius follows the forest track, advancing along the flank of the Kalkrieser Berg.

2 The Bructeri temporarily cease their harassment of the Roman column in order to regroup for a further attack once the Romans encounter the defended rampart.

3 As his scouts report a fork in the track, Eggius advances towards the head of the column to judge the situation for himself and discovers the presence of a defended rampart which threatens any further advance.

4 Eggius detaches half of his command – some six cohorts – to attack and clear the enemy position whilst the remainder adopt a defensive stance whilst waiting for the rest of the column under Caeonius to come up.

5 The six cohorts advance towards the rampart in *testudo* formation in order to defend against enemy missiles, and assault the position by using locked shields as makeshift ramps. Despite gaining a number of footholds the legionaries are unable to break into the German position and after inconclusive hand-to-hand fighting are forced to withdraw and reorganize before launching another attack.

A DESPERATE SITUATION
Morning, 11 September

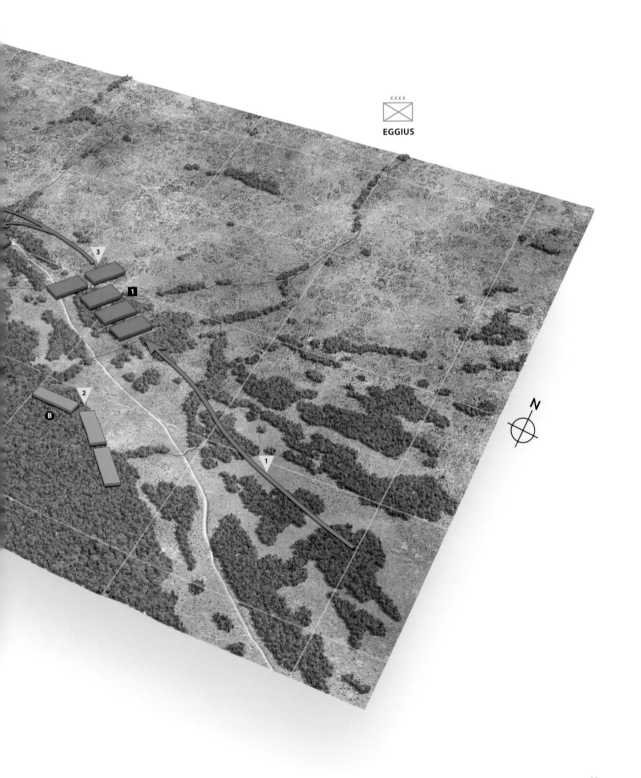

EGGIUS

Within the central section of the battlefield, bio-archaeologists have reproduced the fauna of the 1st century AD to give visitors a better perception of the battlefield in autumn, AD 9.

Within the confines of the forest, the tribesmen, having shadowed the Romans for several kilometres, now began to repeat their spoiling attacks of the previous two days, slowly taking a steady toll of the enemy but also taking casualties from the Roman auxiliary troops who were making limited counterattacks as the more heavily armoured legionaries continued to press forwards. Along the line, orders were now being given that the badly wounded were to be left behind, and many of them were killed by their comrades in order to prevent them from being captured alive. It was by any consideration a callous decision, but undoubtedly a necessary one to make if the army were to survive – to stop within the confines of the forest meant almost certain death. It did not, however, serve to preserve the integrity of the column as holes began to appear in the ranks and individual unit commanders had no time to reorganize their troops who were by now beginning instinctively to bunch up, creating further gaps in the line into which the enemy could launch a sudden attack followed by an equally quick withdrawal to safety.

Further back along the track, Arminius now came upon the abandoned marching camp and, as his men slaughtered the few remaining wounded, he could feel more than satisfied with the progress of the fighting. His personal troops were now within striking distance of the fleeing Romans, and could launch an attack against them should he so choose. Elsewhere messengers had confirmed that the heavy skirmishing was by now causing significant enemy casualties and although the tribesmen's own losses were mounting in the face of Varus' changed tactics it was a matter of no great import. A reduction in the strength of potentially hostile factions could only bolster his position when it came to the unavoidable necessity of choosing a warrior to lead the tribes against the Romans and then, when expedient, against Maroboduus of the Marcomanni who was like a festering sore that needed to be eradicated. Perhaps, he mused, it might not be too bad a thing if the Sugambri were also to receive a bloody nose or two before they cleared the Lippe Valley, for as a Cheruscan noble he could afford to be generous in spending his allies' lives in order to achieve victory. It was now, however, time to bring the fighting to a conclusion. For the Romans, in their despair, to be made aware who was responsible for their destruction.

Although driven by military necessity, Varus' decision to abandon both the camp and the heavily wounded and then to destroy much of the supply train had initially been proved to be the correct choice, as the reduced column had proved easier to control even as the first of the screaming enemy warriors had thrown himself against the marching troops. That had been some hours ago, and now the army had devolved into three distinct bodies all moving semi-independently of each other, though with the same ultimate objective. Each of the three legions had taken on a distinct role. Ahead of Varus, the advance guard was slowly cutting its way through a continual series of ambuscades, followed by the main body of the army centred around his own headquarters, whilst behind him the rearguard – now joined by Vala's troopers – attempted to shepherd the remaining baggage forwards through the morass left in the wake of the leading elements. In spite of this dogged progress, however, the command structure was slowly breaking down. Although Varus could issue orders and receive reports from the troops in his immediate vicinity, with the narrow track completely blocked by the marching troops it was virtually impossible for couriers to move between the three main elements without forcing the army to come to a halt.

The reconstruction of the German rampart has been made in two sections. To the left of the picture, the ground has been excavated to the original ground level of AD 9 and is enclosed by a wall of steel girders, whilst to the right it has been rebuilt at the present ground level, with only the dried withies standing out against the forest backdrop to mark its location.

With the forest swarming with the enemy, to leave the path was to invite certain death whilst – however important the message – a rider trying to force his way through the mass of bodies would only disrupt the column and perhaps cause a fatal delay. It was a credit to Arminius' planning that even when his actual location was unknown, he was still dictating events from afar, for whilst the slowly moving column was tied to the forest track, all Varus and his army could do was to plod forwards, trusting that the vanguard would sweep the enemy aside and open up a route to the next area of open terrain where a marching camp could be built and the troops rested and reorganized before the next stage of the march was embarked upon.

Veering to the north-west, the head of the Roman column broke out of the forest during the early afternoon, the men, thankful that they could now re-form for battle as they had been trained to do, finding comfort in the familiar formations and covering the successive units as they debouched, battered and bloodied, from the tree line. Having successfully mauled the Roman column for several hours, the German attacks were by now slackening off. The tribesmen had already had their victory and saw no advantage in courting death by engaging the Romans in the open. For Varus, however, there was no time for relief, as looking around at his battered troops his sole priority became to find a defensible area where he could construct a new laager behind the ramparts of which his men could bind their wounds and prepare for the following day's march and, while the troops moved off at a slow pace, mounted scouts were sent ahead to find a suitable campsite.

In his book *In Quest of the Lost Legions*, his account of his discovery and subsequent exploration of the Kalkriese battlefield, Major Tony Clunn makes an eloquent case for the location of Varus' final encampment as being the Felsenfeld near the village of Schwagstorf, some kilometres to the east of Kalkriese. The high escarpment dominates the local area and would have been the perfect site upon which Varus could build a marching camp where he could reconsider his options. When looking for a suitable location for a camp, the Romans invariably sought an area of rising ground, which would not only have natural drainage but would also add to the height advantage enjoyed by the defenders, the Felsenfeld not only meets both of these criteria, but is also the meeting point of several routes both through the forest and across the Weihengebirge, the long ridge of high ground which formed the left flank of Varus' march westwards. For the commander of the shattered column it must have seemed like a gift from the gods, if his troops could survive one more night, then perhaps they could seize the initiative, no longer being shepherded along the forest paths like lambs to the slaughter.

With horsemen deployed to cover the approaches to the encampment, the defences slowly took shape, and, as the work progressed, Varus once again met with his senior officers to ascertain the condition of the various units and to make plans for the following day. Looking around the tent, it was clear that the situation was not good. The army's ranks had been thinned by the incessant fighting of the last few days and indeed most of the men present had been wounded to some degree, but perhaps the most damning indictment of all was the absence of the legates of *legiones XVII* and *XIIX*, both of whom had been killed during the march. Although the centurions were busily compiling casualty lists, by purely looking about the camp it was clear to all that despite its having given a good account of itself, the army had been severely mauled in the running combat of the previous few days.

Fatigued and possibly bothered by wounds, Varus canvassed those officers present for their assessment of the situation. Opinions were divided – to the west, the track again entered the forest and, given the inevitability of further attack, many felt that the army would not survive another day's march like that which had just ended. There seemed to be a pass through the hills to the south that might possibly bring the column closer to Aliso and the Lippe Valley and should be therefore scouted thoroughly. To the north there was also an area of open ground, which should also be investigated as it might allow the army to deploy formally rather than march strung out along the twisting forest paths. As orders were given for scouts to cover both of these areas, the meeting reached its crucial point. Could the army proceed in its present condition? The unanimous answer was a resounding 'yes', and as a man who had once held Rome's senior magistracy, it was the only answer that he had truly expected. Even so, in the tired eyes of his subordinates he must have noticed a certain hesitancy, fatigue and wariness, the first signs that his command was slowly beginning to disintegrate as a unit.

Later that afternoon the scouts returned to camp. To the south, the pass over the hills was rough going and, given the previous days' bad weather, in order for the army to make any progress it would require the abandonment of all the remaining wheeled transport, and for the seriously wounded to be left behind again to face near-certain death at the hands of the enemy. The flat land to the north, however, seemed more inviting – it appeared that the route was open in the most part and, though waterlogged by the heavy rainfall, it would be kinder to the column than having to plunge through the forest. Admittedly it would take the troops initially further away from safety, but it would at least prevent the enemy from springing further ambushes, removing at least one major problem.

It was then that Varus must have made a crucial decision that would affect both his future and that of the whole army. Summoning Numonius Vala to his tent, he instructed him to take a detachment of cavalry – the fittest of the remaining troopers mounted on the best of the remaining cavalry horses – and to ride north initially and, having bypassed any adverse terrain, eventually swinging westwards towards the Rhine. With the bulk of the Army of Germania Inferior already present in the camp, Varus was fully aware that

This early-type legionary helmet may still have been in service with a number of troops at the beginning of AD 9. Unlike the Coolus type, the crest holder is an integral part of the helmet bowl, whilst on the shortened neck guard two rivets can be seen that would have held in place a small plaque inscribed with the owner's name and unit.

there was no immediate hope of relief. His only realistic option, therefore, was to cut his way through the enemy lines and fight his way to safety, either to the Rhine bases or the lands of Rome's Frisian allies, who might be prevailed upon to march to Varus' rescue as they had once saved Augustus' stepson Drusus.

The premise was not an unreasonable one – both sides had been badly bloodied during the running battle of the past few days, but whereas the Romans could shelter nightly behind their ramparts, to some degree protected by their tents from the elements, the enemy warriors were exposed to the wind and rain. Whilst the Romans, if they husbanded their resources adequately, had supplies for several days – and indeed could, if necessary, resort to eating their pack mules – the Germans had to forage for food and would soon have exhausted the supplies in the immediate vicinity, meaning that they could not remain as concentrated as they had previously been. With the facts available to hand, and like many Romans an inveterate gambler, Varus must still have felt that the odds favoured a Roman break-out.

As Varus' legate in Germania Inferior, once he had reached safety Vala's primary mission was to warn the outlying outposts in Germania Magna of the danger and, if necessary, organize a limited withdrawal to the Rhine, redeploying the meagre forces available into a defensive posture whilst awaiting further instructions or reinforcements. Upon reaching the Ems he was to send messengers to the Frisii asking them to march to relieve Varus. The situation permitting, Nonius Asprenas in Moguntiacum could detach one of his two legions to reinforce Vetera, but there was no way of knowing how far Arminius' treachery had spread, which tribes were loyal and which hostile. Varus believed that at best the position in Upper Germany would be stable and peaceful, and, although Asprenas' forces could already be heavily engaged, there was still no question that the situation had as yet deteriorated out of control, and that the Army of Germania Inferior would be unable to fight its way out of its present predicament.

His preparations completed, Vala led his small force out of the camp and the troopers began to pick their way northwards. All eyes in the camp were on the riders as they slowly began to disappear from view, but then from the east came what could only be a large body of enemy horsemen, many amongst them clearly wearing Roman equipment, and who, kicking their horses forwards, slowly began to overhaul the fleeing cavalrymen. Their mounts tired and jaded, and themselves exhausted after the long march, the Roman troopers were quite simply overwhelmed by the enemy numbers, many of them stunned and shocked by the realization that they were dying at the hands of those that they had believed to be their own allies. Arminius had finally committed his forces to battle, thus closing one of Varus' few remaining options; either the army had to attempt to make a break-out to the south, or continue westwards and try to force its way through the next wave of attacks, hoping to reach more favourable terrain or inflict sufficient losses to encourage the enemy to withdraw.

The destruction of Vala's command marked a distinct change in the situation of the Roman column. Until now there had always been the chance that the Rhine bases could be given sufficient warning to defend themselves, and perhaps this was one blow too many for Varus to take. A possible combination of wounds, fatigue, the fear of capture or maybe even a sense of failure and the desire to save his family honour led him to make a critical decision. Sometime during this, the final evening of the march, and aided by a body servant, Varus took his own life in the traditional manner, by falling on his sword. According to Paterculus (Book II, Ch. cxix): 'The General had more courage to die than to fight, for, following the example of his father and grandfather, he ran himself through with his sword'.

This plate on the Weg der Römer near the base of the rampart, marks the location where the skeleton of one of the Roman pack mules was found. Attached to its harness was a large bronze bell, which had previously been muffled. It is believed that around 80 pack animals met their end in or around this location.

To the modern mind this would undoubtedly be referred to as 'the coward's way out', but to the Romans such an act does not have the same stigma attached to it. Instead of an act of despair, it is on one hand an act of atonement, an acceptance of blame. On the other hand it is also an attempt to salvage some pride and honour from a blatantly lost cause. We know that Varus' father, having fought on the losing side at Philippi, took his own life before the victors could impose any proscriptions, hoping to preserve his son's inheritance. Likewise, Varus would also have viewed the taking of his own life as a reasonable price to pay for *his* son's not paying for the sins of the father. Dio (Book 56, Ch. 21) subsequently implies that once the news of Varus' death had become common currency amongst the unit commanders, a number of them followed his dubious example 'And so Varus and all the senior officers, fearing that they would either be taken alive or slaughtered by their bitterest enemies – for they had already been wounded – nerved themselves for the dreaded but unavoidable act, and took their own lives'. The inevitability of their choosing 'death before dishonour' is clear, but at least two of the senior officers, Lucius Eggius and Caeonius, the camp prefects – *praefecti castrorum* – of *legiones XVII* and *XIIX* were still alive the following morning to lead the army into its final battle.

Memorial plate forming part of the Weg der Römer commemorating three known casualties of the battle – the legionary Marcus Aius, the centurion Marcus Caelius and the imperial legate, Publius Quinctilius Varus.

THE FINAL MARCH, 11 SEPTEMBER

With the full weight of command descending on their shoulders, Caeonius and Eggius had scant time to decide what to do next. Although the suicides of both Varus and a number of their colleagues had severely debilitated the army's chain of command, it was in fact the death of Numonius Vala that afternoon that caused them the most problems. The arrival of the enemy to the north of the encampment had not only closed a possible avenue of escape, but had also brought home to them the fact that this was no isolated insurrection but rather a calculated uprising. One that was led – at least in part – by one of their own officers, albeit one who had originally been a hostage in Rome.

TOP LEFT
This view eastwards follows the Weg der Römer back towards Eggius' initial position, before he launched the desperate attack on the rampart. The orange stakes to the left of the picture indicate locations where artefacts have been found.

TOP RIGHT
Bells attached to their harness allowed the muleteers not only to keep track of their charges, but also served to reassure the other pack animals that there was no danger. This bronze example, found near the German rampart, had been muffled with grass in order not to inadvertently warn the tribesmen of the Roman position. (AKG Images/ Varusschlacht Museum, Kalkriese)

BOTTOM
The row of metal stakes shown here follows the line of the German rampart. To the left of the image is the Pavilion Hören (Hearing) – one of three fixed exhibits on the battlefield that show the visitor how our senses can easily become disoriented on the battlefield. The other two exhibits are Fragen (Questioning) and Sehen (Seeing).

The Weg der Römer looking eastwards back towards the museum building. It was roughly from this spot that the prefect, Lucius Eggius, would have made his decision to assault the German rampart.

In considering the choices remaining available to them, the two officers would have realized that, in fact, they had no choices at all. The north was now closed to them, whilst the route south across the Weihengebirge, if taken, would have been tortuous enough for the able-bodied soldiers in the column, let alone the wounded. It would also have been obvious to them that enemy forces were converging on their position and that to remain encamped where they were would only serve to invite defeat. Although it was certain that by continuing their advance they would inevitably become embroiled in another running combat, it would not be against fresh troops, but rather against men who had, like them, been fighting non-stop over the past few days, and who again had also taken significant losses during that time. If they could only bludgeon their way through the next series of enemy positions, then perhaps a chance still remained that the battered remnants of the army could be saved.

Given the losses over the last few days and the, by now, largely non-existent baggage train it is possible that the usual order of march was abandoned and the army was now re-formed into two 'battlegroups' based around the survivors of *legiones XVII* and *XIIX*, commanded by Caeonius and Eggius respectively, with the remnants of *legio XIX* and any remaining auxiliaries being allocated between these two ad hoc formations. The reason for this assumption is that these two men are the only senior officers mentioned by the contemporary sources as having survived Varus' final evening, suggesting that some form of joint command had devolved upon their shoulders. We know that Caedicius, their colleague in *legio XIX* was now commanding at Aliso and the fact that the men are mentioned by name would seem to indicate that all of the other senior officers had – by this time – either been killed in action or had followed Varus' example and taken their own lives. The command of *legio XIX* should, in theory, have devolved upon one of the lesser tribunes who, as a member of the minor nobility, should have been mentioned by either Paterculus, Florus or Dio and this omission would support an assertion that its command element had been particularly badly hit in the fighting to date and that the only real option for it to continue functioning as a combat unit would have been to split the surviving cohorts amongst its sister legions.

That evening, as the two men made their plans for the following day's march, the bodies of the dead were interred together, the sole exception being Varus whose body was laid in a separate hole in the ground and cremated. However, before the flames could take hold, the makeshift grave was quickly filled with earth and the half-burned corpse partially buried. With the funeral rites for their late commander duly observed, the two officers completed their preparations for the following morning.

Given Paterculus' later comments, it would seem that Eggius led the first of the battlegroups and with the discovery of a bell from a pack mule that had been muffled with grass and plants, it would be a reasonable assumption that he tried to repeat the earlier tactic of commencing the day's march before daybreak in order to make as much progress as possible before his movement was detected by the enemy. Following the track, the 4,000 or so men attempted to maintain as tight a formation as possible before plunging into

This view of the rear of the reconstructed German rampart clearly shows the constricted fighting platform, which could have been manned only by a single rank of warriors. In the centre of the picture we can see one of the 'sally ports', which would have undoubtedly been barricaded before the defenders launched their own counterattack.

GÖTTERDÄMMERUNG (pp. 74–75)

Faced with the threat of the enemy position flanking his – by now constricted – line of march, the prefect Lucius Eggius had no other option than to storm the German rampart, in an attempt to protect the succeeding elements of the army.

In this scene, one of the centuries, having approached the rampart *in testudo*, has now expanded its formation to allow the legionaries to bombard the enemy with missiles **(1)** whilst a number of men use the roof of locked shields as a ramp **(2)** to come into contact with the enemy, some using *dolabrae* and other entrenching tools **(3)** in an attempt to cut their way into the German position, whilst others engage the defending tribesmen 'hand to hand' as a way of shielding their comrades **(4)**.

With the assaulting troops unable to make any real impression upon the newly constructed palisade **(5)**, which simply bows

under the pressure of the axemen, the attack is doomed to failure and Eggius is obliged to call off the assault and pull his men back to reorganize themselves for a second attack. With the destruction of Caeonius' force, and the fugitives of *legio XIIX* now disrupting Eggius' position, it was the beginning of the end for Varus' proud army. All that remained was to attempt a final, and in the end futile, break-out that saw Eggius' troops collapse under overwhelming numbers of the enemy. Only a few of the battered and bleeding legionaries were to survive this last enemy attack, fleeing for the dubious safety of the forest. Here, shrouded by the undergrowth, most of them were to die a lonely death, succumbing to their wounds, unseen by friend and foe alike, whilst even fewer made their way to the Rhine and safety, traumatized by the bloodbath that they had so narrowly escaped.

rough terrain once more. Again, orders were that any wounded were to be left behind in order not to impede the progress of the main body. Once Eggius' command was suitably under way, Caeonius and the second group were to abandon the camp, following in their comrades' wake.

Elsewhere, and some kilometres to the south-east, Arminius was finalizing his own plans for the destruction of Varus' army. Although his allies would continue to harass the Roman column, the majority of the warriors would now take up position behind the rampart on the lower slopes of the Kalkrieser Berg, a large northern-facing spur of high ground that abuts the Weihengebirge near Kalkriese, reinforcing the bottleneck with the Grosse Moor, the Great Moor.

Although not Cheruscan, these tribesmen would have perhaps the most crucial role in this final battle. Their presence in strength on the enemy's flank would mean that the legionaries would be unable to ignore the latent threat and would be forced to attack the rampart in order to keep their escape route open. Unless they could achieve this, the army would be stopped dead in its tracks allowing Arminius' own warriors to fall upon and destroy the rearguard in detail. The Romans would therefore be trapped between the two wings of a numerically superior enemy and simply crushed 'between a rock and a hard place'.

Exhausted by their exertions of the last few days, the warriors had indeed inflicted significant losses upon the enemy but, it must be noted, they too had taken casualties and, without shelter from the elements had also been unable to light many fires over the preceding evenings unless they should give their numbers and positions away to the enemy. Cold and undoubtedly hungry they waited for the dawn to come and bring them victory over the proud legions.

Close-up of rampart showing the interweaving of the withies between a line of stakes to form a flexible defensive wall, rising perhaps to the defenders' upper torso. Again, notice should be taken of the narrowness of the fighting platform.

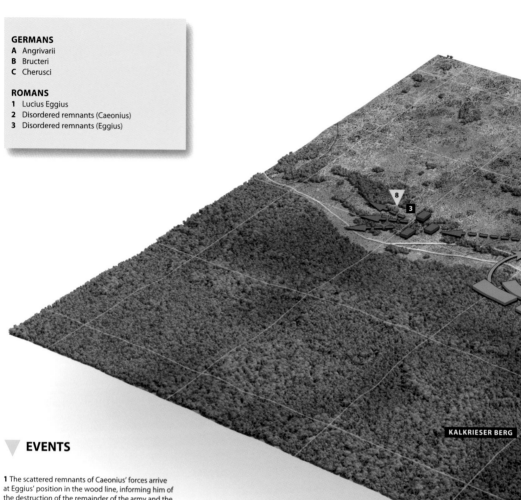

GERMANS
A Angrivarii
B Bructeri
C Cherusci

ROMANS
1 Lucius Eggius
2 Disordered remnants (Caeonius)
3 Disordered remnants (Eggius)

KALKRIESER BERG

▼ EVENTS

1 The scattered remnants of Caeonius' forces arrive at Eggius' position in the wood line, informing him of the destruction of the remainder of the army and the presence of large numbers of enemy troops to his rear.

2 Eggius recalls the attacking cohorts, and the reunited command forms up en masse in an attempt to bludgeon their way through to safety.

3 With the pressure on them relieved, the Angrivarii now launch a counterattack from behind the rampart. Numbers of warriors sally out through a number of gates in the palisade but the majority sweep westwards around the defences and block the Roman advance.

4 The Bructeri now advance from their positions on the Kalkrieser Berg and attack the Roman column from the rear.

5 The remnants of the Army of Germania Inferior make slow progress against the Angrivarian warriors and by now forced to meet the threat from the Bructeri, Eggius' column grinds to a halt.

6 Having looted the Roman camp on the Felsenfeld and put the survivors to the sword, Arminius and the Cheruscans arrive from the east and throw their weight against the Roman position.

7 Heavily outnumbered, and with the numbers of dead and wounded increasing steadily, Eggius' position collapses and the men are overrun.

8 Small groups of fugitives manage to escape the massacre and flee westwards. Many are overtaken by enemy warriors or succumb to their wounds and die in the forest, a scant few possibly reach the Rhine and safety.

DEATH IN THE FOREST
Afternoon, 11 September

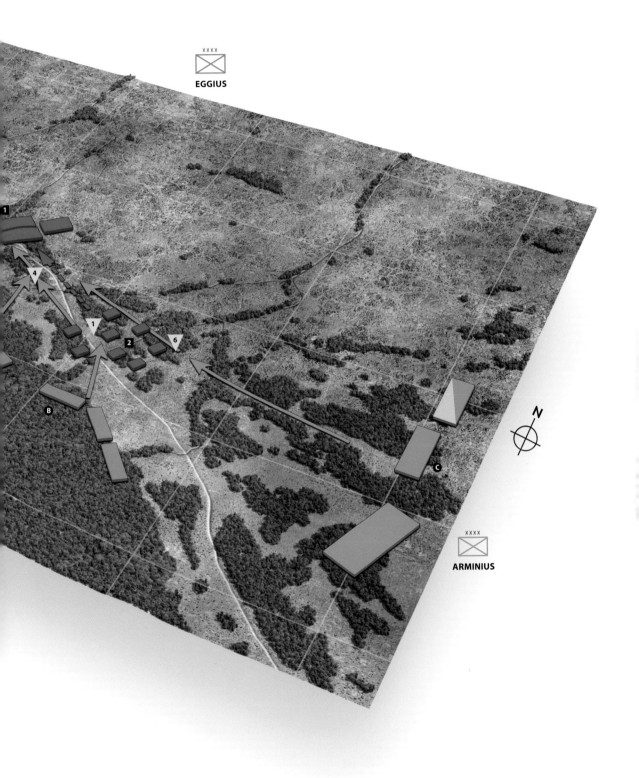

XXXX
EGGIUS

XXXX
ARMINIUS

ABOVE
The raw materials – withies such as these were used by the Germans to provide a flexible defensive wall atop the rampart which the Romans were unable to breach with their axes and entrenching tools.

RIGHT
As part of the reconstruction of the rampart down to the original ground level, bio-archaeologists have reintroduced examples of plants etc for which traces have been found during the excavation to show the terrain as it most likely was in the summer of AD 9.

Sometime before daybreak, Eggius' command stood to, and began the march west. Unseen by the enemy, they initially made good time, but, inevitably once the column reached the next area of forest, progress slowed considerably, so much so that orders were perhaps given that obstacles would no longer be cleared out of the way, and instead the troops would have to negotiate them as best they could. The sands of time were running out and the formation could not afford to halt every hundred or so metres so that a fallen tree could be dragged from the path. As the sun rose and visibility within the forest improved, the troops grew increasingly apprehensive of enemy attacks but as the legionaries marched deeper and deeper into the woods nothing happened. After sending scouts out to investigate the terrain ahead, Eggius called a halt in order to marshal together any stragglers. He then sent a runner back to Caeonius at the camp on the Felsenfeld, informing him of the unit's position and urging him to make best possible speed in order to close the gap between them.

It was probably mid-morning when the scouts returned. Having obeyed orders to remain in concealment, they had not pressed too far ahead but were able to advise Eggius that, 2km (1 mile) or so distant, as the woods began to thin out, the pathway forked with one track winding its way along the bottom of the ridgeline that had been on their left flank ever since leaving the summer camp on the Weser, whilst the other route continued more or less directly westwards. Trusting that Caeonius would soon be following in his footsteps, the prefect gave the word that the advance was to resume and then followed the scouts to the head of the column, intent on making his own appraisal. As he reached the tree line, Eggius scanned the route ahead, trying to decide the most likely points from which the enemy could spring another of their interminable ambushes. As he studied the ground, he considered the reason for the two pathways – the fact the one ran along slightly higher ground told him that it was the only one that could be used all year round whilst the other crossed terrain at risk of flooding or inundation. As the marching column was considerably wider than the track, his main concern was now whether or not the recent rainstorms had rendered the lower of the

Eggius' view of his final battlefield. Barely discernable against the tree line, the earthern rampart would have served to funnel the Romans into a narrow area, stretching northwards towards the Great Bog, the edge of which would in all probability have been near the light green marker towards the right of the image adjacent to the line of steel girders.

Rear-facing view of the German rampart showing in detail the manner in which the defensive palisade was constructed. Again, notice should be taken of the narrow walkway that would have limited the number of warriors available to engage the Roman column.

two routes impassable. It was then that he slowly became aware of an anomaly to the left, on the lower hill slopes. It was some distance ahead, but the longer he looked, the more he was certain that he was looking at something that he had seen virtually every day of his military service and indeed, as his legion's engineering specialist, he would have ordered the construction of himself. Albeit rudimentarily camouflaged, it was now clear that the enemy had built an earth rampart parallel to the track. The answers to all of his unspoken questions came all at once – the area around the right-hand path was indeed flooded and by building the rampart the enemy had created an artificial bottleneck through which the column would have to force its passage.

GÖTTERDÄMMERUNG, 11 SEPTEMBER

Coming quickly to a decision, Eggius saw that if the remnants of the army were to survive, he could not afford to ignore the barricade. It had obviously been constructed with a clear purpose in mind and therefore only its capture or destruction could serve to thwart the enemy's plans. No longer having any artillery support, his plan was quite simple: whilst the bulk of his men reduced their perimeter in the forest, four cohorts – in parallel column of centuries – would march out into the gap between the forked pathways and, after facing to the left, would form *testudo* – a Roman defensive formation whose name derives from the Latin for tortoise – again by centuries. The leading cohorts would now advance towards the enemy, and when they reached the rampart the flanks of the *testudo* would open outwards, with the troops bombarding the defenders with missiles. Those legionaries whose shields had formed the roof of the formation would use them to form a ramp, up which the rear ranks – partially equipped with *dolabrae*, Roman entrenching tools, almost a cross between an axe and a mattock, and other engineering tools – would attack the palisade, attempting to force a breach into which supporting troops could then advance. The remaining cohort would act as a reserve, providing support as needed but also cover should the enemy make a sudden counterattack.

By now aware that the Roman advance troops were assaulting the barricade, Arminius began his final preparations to launch the decisive attack on Caeonius' column as it brought up the enemy rear. Waiting until the legionaries were several hundred metres away from the abandoned camp, the Cheruscan war leader rose in his saddle and gave the signal for the tribesmen concealed on the slopes of the Ostercappeln Hills to strike down at the left flank of the marching troops, whilst the mixed force that had prevented Vala's escape the previous afternoon now came thundering in against their open right flank.

Heavily outnumbered by the charging warriors, many of the exhausted legionaries were cut down in this short and vicious combat, which saw Caeonius' command shattered by the sudden attack. As they recoiled from the assault, the prefect led the small group of men around him back towards the Felsenfeld, hoping to find shelter and protection behind the walls of the stockade that they had earlier abandoned. Those survivors who had had the dubious honour of having led the march now fled west, hoping to find safety with Eggius' troops whilst the vast majority of the legionaries lay scattered in isolated knots, the wounded, the dead and the dying simply overwhelmed by the enemy numbers.

Satisfied with the destruction around him, Arminius allowed his men to vent their emotions on the wreckage of the Roman column, picking his way through the carnage whilst scanning the ranks of the dead for signs of his nemesis, Varus. Content to let the fugitives escape and cause havoc amongst the Roman vanguard, he barked a sharp series of orders and, flanked by his auxiliaries and a large body of warriors, made his way back to the Felsenfeld certain that his prey cowered behind the palisade, confident in the knowledge that the pitiful few who had escaped from this part of the battlefield would be unable to defend their final encampment.

As his force approached the stockade, Arminius sent a small group of his auxiliaries forwards to offer the senior Roman officer a safe conduct to parley. It was an offer that Caeonius with only a few hundred – mostly wounded – survivors of his legion under arms could only accept.

Standing in the shadow of the *porta praetoria*, he waited as Arminius and a mounted escort approached the camp, and, as they drew level, the German asked one simple question: 'Where is Varus?' Exhausted, Caeonius turned and gestured for Arminius to follow as he re-entered the camp, walking towards a small pile of freshly turned earth. Ordering some of his men to secure the gate, Arminius signalled to the Cheruscan war-band and then rode into the camp, following the Roman officer. After some moments, Caeonius indicating the small mound answered the question he had been posed, 'There lies Varus', he intoned unemotionally. Pausing to reflect for a moment, Arminius turned to face his warriors who had now seized the camp's main gate, and with a single barked command the killing began again, any pleas for mercy being drowned out by the cries of the dying and the wounded. When the last Roman had died and silence reigned over the charnel house, a number of warriors dug down where Caeonius had indicated, and, roughly dragging the half-burned corpse into the daylight, soon presented their chieftain with the severed head of his bitterest foe, the symbol of Roman domination.

At the other entrance to the pass and unaware of the fate of their comrades, Eggius' cohorts had launched their own, desperate, attack on the German barricade. Protected by the interlocked shields that gave the tortoise-like formation its name, the legionaries slowly made their way to the enemy position and, as the flanking infantry opened their formation to launch a barrage of missiles at the defenders, the assault parties rushed up the makeshift ramps, throwing themselves at the palisade, trying to tear a hole in the plashing through which supporting troops could charge into the enemy ranks beyond. At first, the tactic seemed to work admirably with several footholds being secured at the top of the rampart and one section even collapsing under the weight of the combatants, but as the axes and *dolabrae* were swung at the interwoven branches, the wooden mesh only bowed and bent under the force of the blows rather than breaking or splitting. It was soon clear that no substantial breach could be cut through the withies and that if they were to survive, the Romans would have to cut their way through the wall of living flesh that sought to prevent their escape. With many of their number forming the human ramps, it soon became an unequal contest for the legionaries – the enemy could replace their casualties in the fighting line almost as soon as they were inflicted, whilst their own losses mounted steadily. Unable to make any impact on the German defences, they withdrew out of missile range to regroup and reorganize themselves.

Then, from behind them came a cry of despair as the bloodied remnants of their sister legion flooded into Eggius' perimeter. As the more coherent of the fugitives began hurriedly to explain Arminius' treachery and the utter rout of Caeonius' troops, it became clear to the prefect that the rampart had indeed done its job by keeping him and his men busy whilst their comrades were slaughtered. Further attempts to storm the barricade would simply result in unnecessary deaths when there was now only one realistic option available to him – to gather his troops and force his way through to the west and safety, trusting in the tribesmen's indiscipline and desire for plunder overriding the military necessity of crushing the last remnants of Varus' ill-fated army. Placing himself by the legion's *aquila* Eggius snapped an order to the few remaining musicians and, as the trumpet calls sounded, the survivors of the Army of Germania Inferior began to form themselves into a compact mass before setting off at a jog-trot, each man focused on the back of the man ahead.

With the pressure released, small groups of warriors picked their way through the gaps in the rampart and, as the Romans began to move away, javelins, stones and other missiles rained down on the battered legionaries. As their confidence grew so their numbers increased and reinforced by Arminius and his Cheruscans who had, by now, completed the destruction of the camp on the Felsenfeld, they began to launch a series of sustained attacks on the column, bringing it eventually to a complete standstill, the numbers of their foes ever dwindling until a final knot of men, their *aquila* held defiantly aloft, stood surrounded, prepared to sell their lives dearly. As their comrades fell a handful of survivors, those who had been at the very front of the column, stumbled through the concealing undergrowth, twisting this way and that as they sought to distance themselves from the enemy pursuit, intent on escaping the field of carnage behind them. With Varus' gory visage held aloft as a talisman, Arminius surveyed the battlefield, perhaps disbelieving that the army that inflicted defeat after defeat upon his forefathers had now been brought to that same pass. Three legions, over half the Roman army on the Rhine, had been destroyed and the blow to Roman prestige was one from which it might not recover. As his men began to loot the dead or assemble their prisoners for their uncertain fate, he handed Varus' head to one of his retainers, instructing that it be taken to his great rival, Maroboduus of the Marcomanni.

We will never be certain whether Arminius' gesture was intended as a call to arms or a challenge to one of his greatest rivals, but Maroboduus refused to react as Arminius had hoped. Instead, the carefully packed relic was sent post-haste to Rome, perhaps adding more fuel to the fires of revenge that would soon burn in the heart of the empire.

THE AFTERMATH

As news of Varus' defeat spread, a number of those German tribes that had previously been lukewarm in their relations with Arminius now acceded to his call to rise up and attack the Roman forts and encampments within their territory, all of which – with a single exception – were quickly overwhelmed and their garrisons slaughtered. The sole outpost to survive was the camp at Aliso where the Roman forces under the command of Lucius Caedicius managed to beat off a number of attacks before conducting a fighting withdrawal to the Rhine.

The Roman response, AD 9

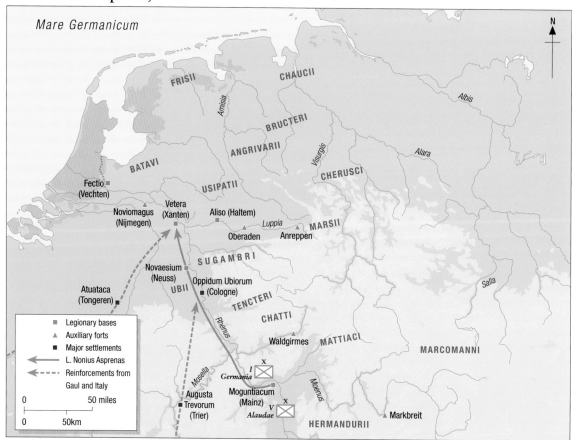

The Roman response, AD 14–16

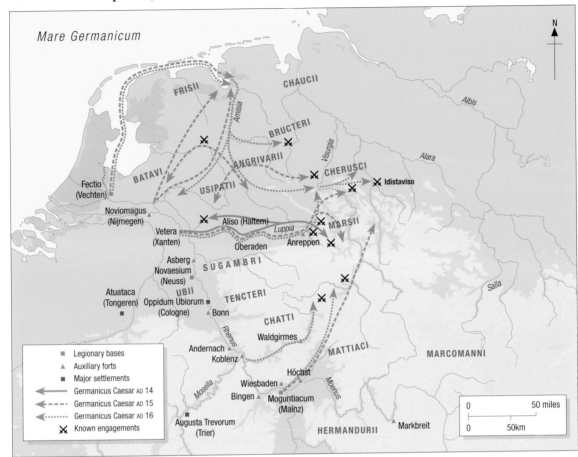

Despite the shock that reverberated from the disaster, the situation in Germania Inferior, whilst acute, was in no way critical, as the sole crossing point on the Rhine – the pontoon bridge at Vetera – could be easily cut loose from the moorings at its eastern end and drawn back across the river in order to deny its use to the enemy. Without a mass of small boats to transport his men Arminius was unable to threaten Roman territory directly. Additionally, the fact that he failed to move against either the Batavi or the Frisii, both tribes that were allied to Rome, seems to indicate a lack of available manpower, possibly a reflection of his own heavy losses in the running battles in the Teutoburger Wald.

Based on the limited amount of intelligence available to them, the Romans reacted as best they could. From Moguntiacum, Asprenas immediately marched north at the head of his two legions, whilst in Rome itself, and Suetonius' description of a distraught Emperor Augustus banging his head against the walls of the Imperial Palace notwithstanding, the initial panic that had seen waves of anti-German hysteria – leading to the expulsion of the imperial bodyguard amongst others from the city – soon gave way to a mood of resignation and determination. Almost immediately the government began the task of mobilizing and equipping both reserve and ad hoc units to strengthen the remaining troops scattered along the Rhine. These, however, were only temporary measures and in the succeeding months an additional

Against all religious considerations – as one of Rome's high priests he was forbidden to visit a battlefield – Augustus' step-grandson, Germanicus visited the battlefield in AD 15 and arranged for the remains of Varus' army to be reinterred. This may account for the examples where both human and animal remains have been recovered from the same site. Woodcut, 1855, after a drawing by Theodor Grosse (1829–91). (AKG Images)

six legions, together with significant numbers of auxiliaries, were transferred from stations throughout the empire to the German military districts. Indeed, by the latter part of AD 10, almost one-third of Rome's military strength had been redeployed to cover the Rhine frontier.

It was also about this time that Augustus ordered the removal of the three legion numbers – *XVII*, *XIIX* and *XIX* – from the army list, never to be reused. On the surface, the generally accepted grounds for this collective punishment revolves around the loss of the three *aquilae* within which, it was believed, resided the spirit of the legions, yet with this punitive disgrace Augustus was setting rather than following precedent. Within living memory, and aside from the *clades Variana* – the Varian disaster; there had been a number of occasions when legions had lost their *aquilae* in combat, ranging from the disaster at Carrhae in 53 BC, where seven of Crassus' legionary eagles were taken by the Parthians, to the Sugambrian raid in 16 BC which saw *legio V Alaudae* defeated and its standard captured. In all instances, the lost insignia were later recovered – those taken both at Carrhae and during Mark Antony's disastrous campaign of 40–38 BC were returned by Parthia by treaty in 20 BC whilst the last of Varus' eagles was itself recaptured in AD 41 – but it was only in this latter case that a collective punishment or indeed any form of censure was imposed. A possible explanation for this is that whilst during the later Republic the legions were more readily identified with their commanding general, Augustus had skilfully redirected this loyalty to both

the Head of State and the Commander-in-Chief, two positions that he himself occupied, following his reduction and reorganization of the army after Actium. Therefore the public disgrace of the defeated legions could be seen as a condemnation of their having 'failed' in their duty to Rome.

By this stage it was clear that Roman territory was in no immediate danger from Arminius or his allies, but this massive redeployment of troops to the Rhine frontier brings into question the oft-repeated assertion that the elderly and, by now, ailing Augustus intended that the Rhine would become the empire's northernmost boundary. The command along the Rhine was now effectively shared between Tiberius and his nephew, Germanicus, but by AD 13 with Augustus in ill health and as the heir was needed in the capital to ensure a smooth succession, Tiberius returned to Rome with Germanicus assuming sole command on the frontier.

Having now distanced himself from any responsibility for the disaster, Augustus then proceeded to act in a manner that would seem to be at variance with his condemnation of the legions. Of all the troops that marched eastwards from Vetera in the late spring of AD 9, the fate of the officers and men, the teamsters and the noncombatants remains a matter of conjecture with one single and notable exception. When Varus' disembodied head was presented to Maroboduus of the Marcomanni, the German chieftain immediately ordered it to be sent to Rome where Augustus ordered that it be interred within his family's vault with all due honour and ceremony. It may be that this reaction was due to familial ties, but at the time when Varus' posterity could easily have been blackened, the Emperor publically refrained from vilifying at least one of the fallen.

As such this is the only concrete evidence that we have for the fate of a member of the Army of Germania Inferior. Thanks to the tombstone erected by his brother, we know that the much-decorated centurion, Marcus Caelius, was killed during the running battle but have no way of knowing exactly how this valiant soldier, or indeed the majority of his comrades, met their end. Similarly we can only surmise that the three cohorts left behind to

After the battle, much of the army's impedimenta were strewn across the battlefield. These examples of Roman tools serve as a reminder that the legion was not simply an instrument of war but also one of peace whose engineering skills were often brought into use on behalf of the state.

garrison the bases at Oppidum Ubiorum, Novaesium and Vetera, along with Lucius Caedicius and the troops that he managed to extricate from the fall of Aliso, were simply redistributed amongst those units then being redeployed to the Rhine frontier, all memory of their former postings being eradicated from the official records. As to the inevitable number of prisoners taken by the Germans, sources would indicate that significant numbers were tortured and then executed by their captors as part of religious ceremonies, their remains strewn across the forest. We have no way of gauging the truth of these assertions and, whilst likely, they are by no means definite as the first accounts of the battle were only written two decades after the event, a time in which any surviving prisoners could have died.

The accession of Tiberius in AD 14 saw increasing levels of unrest amongst the Rhine legions, and when the troops in Germania Inferior mutinied against the new regime, Tacitus (*Annals, Book 1, Ch. 31–54*) tells us that Germanicus led them in a pre-emptive strike along the valley of the Lippe, apparently to vent their spleen against the enemy rather than against their own government Despite the reasons behind it, and although it was not crowned with a battlefield victory, Germanicus' raid could still be viewed with some satisfaction by the Emperor when Rome's confidence and martial reputation were in some way restored with the capture of one of the legionary eagles from the Marsii, to whom Arminius had presumably awarded it either in gratitude for their belated support, or as the price of future assistance. Whether or not this was a 'blind' for the beginning of a reconquest of Germania Magna will most likely never be known, but in the summer of AD 15 Germanicus launched a two-pronged attack from Vetera and Moguntiacum that devastated the area between the Ems and the Lippe. On his return journey, during the course of which he had been able to force the return of a second of the captured eagles – this time from the Bructeri, Germanicus must have crossed Varus' earlier route as he came upon the battlefield, still strewn with the wreckage of the fallen army. Ignoring the restrictions placed upon him as a member of the Roman priesthood, Germanicus wandered the battlefield and ordered that his troops reinter their fallen comrades as best they could as, despite the best attentions of his men, it was inevitable after several years that human and animal remains would become intermingled. Before continuing on his westward march, he ordered that a monument be built in honour of Varus' army, but it was a transitory valediction for the dead of the *legiones XVII, XIIX* and *XIX* as it is certain that their remains would have been re-exhumed by the Germans as a tribute to their own pantheon as soon as Germanicus' column was sufficiently far enough distant from the battlefield. Despite this apparent success, the northern wing of the army under Aulus Caecina came under heavy attack and was saved from disaster only when the Germans launched an uncoordinated attack on his camp which was beaten off with heavy losses, allowing the Roman column to extricate itself and return to the Rhine, relatively unscathed.

The following year saw the final stages of the war when Germanicus, despite having heavily defeated Arminius in battle at Idistaviso, on the Weser, was unable to capitalize on his success and was obliged by the lateness of the season to withdraw to winter quarters. Whether or not the Emperor Tiberius had indeed been advised to draw the imperial border along the Rhine is immaterial. As a veteran soldier, he was aware that it had taken over 20 years' hard campaigning against a predominantly disunified enemy to bring Germania Magna under some form of Roman control. Now, however, in the wake of Varus' defeat and with Germanicus unable to secure a comprehensive victory in the field, it was plain to see that a further two decades of fighting – which would see him well into his 70s – would not necessarily bring a successful conclusion to hostilities and the successful integration of a new province into the empire. The cost in resources and manpower, when measured against the potential gain, would simply be too great and so, rather than becoming the springboard for further conquest, the German military districts, with their defences now thickened by an increasing number of fortified encampments, now became the imperial bulwark against *Barbaricum*, effectively becoming provinces themselves. Although future campaigns would be fought – on occasion – across the Rhine, they would be punitive in nature rather than attempts at conquest.

THE BATTLEFIELD TODAY

Following Tony Clunn's initial discoveries, and fuelled by the continued excavation of the Kalkriese site by the local authorities, public interest in the history of the battle grew steadily and in consequence a small information centre was built on the site during the early 1990s. This was later developed into the museum park and, in 2002, a purpose-built museum complex was opened to the public. In 2009, the 2,000th anniversary of the battle was celebrated by a three-tiered exhibition entitled 'Imperium, Konflikt, Mythos' hosted by the museums at Detmold, Haltern and Kalkriese, which gave a multifaceted overview of Roman Germany and which was complemented by the exhibits at museums such as the Römisch-Germanisches Museum in Cologne and the Römermuseum in Xanten. For those who wish to follow the route of Varus and his legions there are a number of hiking trails, such as the Hermannsweg, which traverse the region.

For readers who would be interested in contacting the museum direct, address details are as follows:

Varusschlacht im Osnabrücker Land,
Museum und Park Kalkriese,
Venner Strasse 69,
49565 Bramsche-Kalkriese,
Germany.
Tel: 0049 5468 92040
Email: info@kalkriese-varusschlacht.de
Web: www.kalkriese-varusschlacht.de

BIBLIOGRAPHY

Bähr, Paul, *Die Örtlichkeit der Schlacht auf Idistaviso* Otto Hendel, Halle a.d.: Saale, 1888

Bishop, M. C., and Coulston, J. C. N, *Roman Military Equipment: From the Punic Wars to the fall of Rome* Oxbow Books: Oxford, 2009

Campbell, Duncan B., *Roman Legionary Fortresses 27 BC–AD 378* Osprey Publishing Ltd: Oxford, 2006

——, *Roman Auxiliary Forts 27 BC–AD 378* Osprey Publishing Ltd: Oxford, 2009

Carroll, Maureen, *Romans, Celts & Germans: The German Provinces of Rome* Tempus Publishing: Stroud, 2001

Cheesman, G. L., *The Auxilia of the Roman Imperial Army* Ares Publishers: Chicago, 1975

Clunn, Major J. A. S., *In Quest of the Lost Legions: The Varusschlacht* Minerva Press: London, 1999

Cowan, Ross, *Roman Legionary 58 BC–AD 69* Osprey Publishing Ltd: Oxford, 2003

——, *Roman Battle Tactics 109 BC–AD 313* Osprey Publishing Ltd: Oxford, 2007

Dederich, A., *Kritik der Quellenberichte über die Varianische Niederlage im Teutoburger Walde* Ferdinand Schöning: Paderborn, 1868

Delbrück, Hans, *Geschichte der Kriegskunst im Rahmen der politische Geschichte – Teil II: Die Germanen* Berlin, 1921

Dio, Cassius, *The Roman History: The Reign of Augustus* (trans I. Scott-Kilvert) Penguin Books: London, 1987

Dixon, Karen R., and Southern, Patricia, *The Roman Cavalry, from the First to the Third Century AD* Barnes & Noble: New York, 2000

Eck, Werner, *The Age of Augustus* Blackwell Publishing: Oxford, 2003

Everitt, Anthony, *The First Emperor: Caesar Augustus and the Triumph of Rome* John Murray: London, 2007

Fields, Nic, *Roman Auxiliary Cavalryman AD 14–193* Osprey Publishing Ltd: Oxford, 2006

——, *The Roman Army of the Principate 27 BC–AD 117* Osprey Publishing Ltd: Oxford 2009

The museum devotes a significant number of resources to education. Here a group of schoolchildren are being taught about the construction of the rampart and its effect on the final stages of the battle.

Goldsworthy, Adrian, *The Complete Roman Army* Thames & Hudson: London, 2003

——, *In the Name of Rome: The Men who won the Roman Empire* Phoenix: London, 2007

——, *Caesar: The Life of a Colossus* Phoenix: London, 2006

Holland, Tom, *Rubicon – The Triumph and Tragedy of the Roman Republic* Abacus: London, 2007

Josephus, Flavius, *The Jewish War* (trans. G. A. Williamson) Penguin Books: London, 1960

Judson, Harry Pratt, *Caesar's Army* Ares Publishers: Chicago, 1943

Keppie, Lawrence, *The Making of the Roman Army – From Republic to Empire* Batsford: London, 1984

Le Bohec, Yann, *The Roman Imperial Army* Hippocrene Books: New York, 1995

Mommsen, Theodor, *The Provinces of the Roman Empire* (2 vols) Barnes and Noble: New York, 1996

Murdoch, Adrian, *Rome's Greatest Defeat: Massacre in the Teutoburg Forest* The History Press: Stroud, 2008

Oldfather, William, and Canter, Howard V., *The Defeat of Varus and the German Frontier Policy of Augustus* University of Illinois: Illinois, 1915

Peddie, John, *The Roman War Machine* Grange Books: London, 1997

Ritter-Schaumburg, Heinz, *Hermann der Cherusker: Die Schlacht im Teutoberger Wald und ihre Folgen für die Weltgeschichte* V. M. A. Verlag: Wiesbaden, 2008

Shipley, Frederick, *Velleius Paterculus – Compendium of Roman History and Res Gestae Divi Augusti* William Heinemann Ltd: London, 1929

Southern, Patricia, *Augustus* Routledge: London, 1998

——, *The Roman Army – A Social & Institutional History* Oxford University Press: New York, 2007

Suetonius, *The Twelve Caesars* (trans R. Graves) Folio Society: London, 1995

Sumner, Graham, *Roman Military Clothing (1) 100 BC–AD 200* Osprey Publishing Ltd: Oxford, 2002

Tacitus, *The Annals of Imperial Rome* (trans M. Grant), Penguin Books: London, 1989

Webster, Graham, *The Roman Imperial Army* A&C Black: London, 1979

Wells, Colin M., *The German Policy of Augustus* Clarendon Press, Oxford, 1972

Wells, Peter, *The Battle that Stopped Rome* W. W. Norton, New York, 2004

Wilcox, Peter, *Rome's Enemies (1) Germanics and Dacians* Osprey Publishing Ltd: Oxford, 1982

INDEX

Figures in **bold** refer to illustrations.